SON OF TWO NATIONS
The Memoirs of an Outsider

Edmund Bush

Grosvenor House
Publishing Limited

This book is published by
Grosvenor House Publishing Ltd
Link House
140 The Broadway, Tolworth, Surrey, KT6 7HT.
www.grosvenorhousepublishing.

A CIP record for this book
is available from the British Library

ISBN 978-1-80381-037-9

This book is a revised version of "Let's Mention the War" published in 2015
ISBN 978-1-78148-420-3

Foreword

After a full and varied life I was prompted to write these memoirs for the simple reason that being of mixed origins has given me a broader view of history which I believe will be helpful in reformulating the basis of our current social ethics.

Before going any further, herewith a brief summary of my early years in Germany:

I was born in Berlin in 1924, and registered as a British citizen even though my father was only half German, having been born and brought up in London by a German father and a British mother. My mother however was German, so genetically I am three quarters German.

The choice of the title for this book was influenced by my desire to commemorate my father, and contribute to what I know to have been his views on a United Europe. As for the subtitle, this goes for him as well, because, like me, and due to circumstances beyond our control, he was an outsider simply because when we lived in Germany (and later in Austria) we were known as British, and when we lived in England as German. This is of course the fate of all of those whose parents come from different countries.

The Bush family name only came into existence around 1915 (or early on during the 1st world war), according to my aunt Winnie's booklet *Memories of my Childhood*. This was when my grandmother Esther changed our name from Buch (her deceased husband's name) to Bush, which in view of the very anti-German feelings at that time made life easier both for her and particularly her daughters Winnie and Ena at their school.

Grandmother came from a very respectable bourgeois family by the name of Nash. Her parents had strongly disapproved of her liaison with Peter Buch, a German artist more than 20 years older. So grandmother, who was a very determined character, finally eloped with him.

My grandfather Buch died before I was born, and my father never told us much about him, apart from the fact that he made a living as a lithographic artist illustrating dictionaries, which enabled him to travel and move his family between London and Berlin. One of his commissions involved a visit to Buckingham Palace to copy a picture of Queen Victoria in the year of her Jubilee. We never got to see this, but I do remember a picture of a marching band attributed to him, and a chocolade box cover picture of a little boy and a little girl.

My father was borne with the name Helmuth Buch in London in 1892 and went to school in Wimbledon. After finishing at grammar school his father decided that he was to go into commerce, and arranged for him to take up a position as a trainee with the American Chamber of Commerce in Berlin around 1912. Father was probably bilingual by that time, since the family had stayed in Berlin before during grandfather's engagements there.

When war broke out in 1914 father was still in Berlin, and since according to German law he was German, he was drafted into the army there. He knew nothing about the change of the family name from Buch to Bush which came about shortly after the beginning ot the First World War, and after the death of my grandfather. The anti-German feelings were at that time sufficient to prompt Grandmother to initiate the change in order to avoid harassment of dad's two sisters at their school in London. Father in Berlin knew nothing about this at the time, Indeed, on his engagement announcement to Clara Schmiechen of December 1918 his name is still given as 'Helmuth Buch', and it is not clear when the new family name became operative as far as he was concerned..

My mother's maiden name was Schmiechen. Her father was a picture frame gilder when I last saw him around 1931 on a visit to Berlin with my mother. I remember going to his place of work on a foggy evening, and mother just talking to him at the back door of the workshop where he was employed.

From the various photographs of my grandfather Schmiechen, he appears to have been a jovial and sociable man, a pipesmoker, cardplayer and dog-owner.

My mother Clara was a more serious person, but she could relax with friends and be sociable and cheerful. During her last year at school she had been a 'Wandervogel' ('wanderbird' – poetical allegory to migrating bird), a kind of rambling association for students who wandered through the countryside during weekends or holiday time, spending the nights in student hostels or just haybarns, sometimes singing traditional songs accompanied by mandolin to earn their keep. After she left school, she was trained in haberdashery or millinery. Clara might have met my father Helmuth as a result of her Brother Walter working with him at the American Chamber of Commerce in Berlin. This would probably have been in 1913, when she was 17. When war broke out in 1914, they were already sweethearts, judging from their correspondence. Although father's loyalties must have been divided, the fact that he was in love with a German girl might have helped to sway him to that side, coupled with the fact that according to German law he was German. So when war broke out, he was drafted into the German army and sent to the Eastern front. He was later moved by the German army intelligence to make use of his native English to interrogate English prisoners of war. On one occasion he was smuggled into a German Prisoner of war compound dressed as an English airman in order to glean information about their opinions of German as compared with British aircraft. There is a picture of him taken by one of his comrades showing him in the uniform of a British pilot, surrounded by his German comrades.

Immediately after the end of the war Clara and Helmuth had their official engagement announced, and they married in 1919. My brother Fred was born the following year after my parents had moved to Zillerthalstrasse No 10 in the Pankow district of Berlin, and I was born in 1924. Our home there was in a block of flats opposite an expanse of allotments.

In 1922 my grandmother had come from England to stay at the flat together with father's sister Winnie. At that time father was in trouble with his translating business, which he had started after leaving the American Chamber of Commerce. Inflation was rampant, and all his income went on feeding the family.

Mother was a good manager, but according to aunt Winnie they practically lived on potatoes and cabbage, and even so they often went hungry. Then grandmother ran out of money and had to return to England, leaving Winnie in father's charge on the understanding that he would take her to an acquaintance of hers, a Lutheran Vicar at a place called Unteroewisheim, where she was to stay until other arrangements could be made for her to join her mother in England. Winnie felt very lonely, even though there were plenty of other children to play with. But there was more than enough to eat, since they lived in a farming community. After a while she got used to her new surroundings, and even went along with a local group of Wandervoegel' on a trip around the countryside, singing German folk songs and staying at youth hostels. She remained with the family for two years, until grandmother came to fetch her back to England.

In 1930 father took a job as sales director for Western Electric in Vienna, where he was to market sound-film equipment in Austria and adjacent central European countries.

Acknowledgments

This is not the first time I am indebted to both my wife Marie and my friend Stephen Greenhalgh for reading the draft and making numerous corrections and suggestions for changes and/or improvements to a book of mine, nor is it the first time I took note of some of the latter but rejected others!

I am also indebted to Frau Friederike Fida of Moedling for being instrumental in my re-union with Roland Loewe in 2008, after many years of unsuccessful endeavours on my part to track him down. As a result, I was able to add his account of what happened to him and his parents before, during and after the war.

Finally I want to thank Frau Dr.Lilli Skarabela and Frau Gertrude Moedlhammer, both from the Moedling Literary Society, for their assistance and information about Peter Weiser, the author of one of the books referred to in Part 2, and also for giving me a book about the history of the Jews in Moedling.

Part 1

Scenes from Childhood: How I became a Nazi

Scenes from childhood often surface in our memories like milestones on a journey. The ones described in this part cover my formative years in Moedling, a small town bordering Vienna adjacent to the Vienna Woods, during a time of political upheaval culminating in the annexation of Austria by Germany. These scenes are meant to be seen through the eyes of the child I then was, and I have tried to authenticate them by reporting them as closely as possible to the way I would have done then.

My references to 'Nazis' in this part have to be interpreted in the context of the time as meaning people who supported the NSDAP (National Socialist German Workers Party) and Austrian unification with Germany. At this time the anti-Semitic element of Nazi ideology was not its dominant theme in Austria, and there was no hint of the persecutions to come. 'Sozi' was the term used to describe supporters of the SPOe, (Social democratic Party of Austria), and 'Black' for supporters of the Austrian Catholic/Fascist coalition.

1931

Berlin and Vienna

The sun is shining and I am lying on a blanket in the grass in our garden in Moedling reading a book by Karl May about his adventures with the Apache Indians. It's early in the afternoon, the red currants are ripe, and every now and again I pluck a little bunch and chew the sweet-sour red berries. It's quiet, in the heat there are not a lot of people about. The only sound I can hear is piano music coming from the summerhouse in the next garden behind one of our big walnut trees.

It's quite different here from Berlin, where we used to live in a block of flats with lots of other people, and I used to play in the road in front of the flats, because there was no garden there. On the other side of the road were allotments. The road was not very busy, and was mainly used by horse drawn carts and bicycles, and children were allowed to play on it. Once I ran into a bicycle and got my head through the spokes of the front wheel. The man on the bike was angry, but I was lucky and my head was OK, apart from a few scratches.

One of my brother Fred's schoolmates, who lived in our block, made a deep impression on Fred and me, because he liked eating grubs picked out of rotten apples. He would store them for a while, until he had enough to show us that he really liked eating them. He always asked us to try them too, but we never did.

We lived up on the second floor, and our neighbours were the Schmidts, who were quite old, I think Herr Schmidt was retired. Papa, my father, went to work in an office every day apart from Saturday afternoons and Sundays, and my brother Fred, who is five years older than I, was at school in the mornings apart from Sundays. When my Muttie, my mother, went out shopping, or was busy in the wash kitchen, she would ask the Schmidts to look after me. They used to give me sweets and a model locomotive to play with which was my favourite toy.

Upstairs under the roof was a drying space full of lines of washing belonging to all the people who lived in our block. I was sometimes allowed up there with Muttie when she was hanging up our washing, but I was frightened of a big doll I could see through the bars of one of the lockers where people kept their things. It looked like a real person, so I always stayed close to Muttie when we were up there.

One of our neighbours in the next flat had a swing which was hung from the frame of the door between two rooms. We were allowed to use it when we were invited in to play with their children. The first time I had a swing on it no one had told me to hold on to the ropes, so I fell off backwards and landed on my head. I think I still have a flat spot there now.

Sometimes we all went on picnics together with friends or my uncles and aunts and cousins to a lake called the Wannsee. Fred was taught to swim there by uncle Paul, who is Muttie's brother, and Fred always says that uncle Paul just threw him into the water and he nearly drowned. I don't think uncle Paul really meant to frighten Fred, he was just thinking he would learn swimming more quickly if he had to.

Muttie has another brother called Walter, who is the father of both of our cousins Rolf and Kitty. Uncle Walter gave Kitty a doll's house with an electric lift with a light bulb in it for her birthday. I thought that was really good. Also Rolf had a little tricycle which I once had a ride on together with him.

Sometimes Fred and I would stay in Treptow, which is a district in Berlin, in our grandparents home which was a little wooden house next to a field and some gardens where people grew vegetables. There we were able to play and sometimes we got on to the stage they had built next to the field for people to play music on and we would pretend to be actors in a theatre.

It wasn't always a good time for me, though. Once when I was staying there on my own without Fred, and missing Muttie, I messed my bed one night. My grannie was very angry and spanked me. Then there was another time when Papa and Muttie took me with them for a weekend stay in Brandenburg where they were going to a dance organised by the company Papa worked for. We stayed at a Pension, and when I woke up in the night I realised Muttie and Papa weren't in their bed. I knocked on the other doors in the flat but no one answered, so eventually I went out through the front door down the stone stairs in my nightshirt to the next flat below and rang the bell and again no one answered. Then I crept back into my bed and cried myself to sleep. When I told Papa and Muttie in the morning they made a fuss of me and said how sorry they were. Later we had breakfast with boiled eggs on a shiny silver plate, and that made me feel a lot happier.

Then Papa got a job with an American company called Western Electric in Vienna. We got on to the night express to Vienna, which was the first time I had been on a train with beds in it. Fred and I had a bunk each to ourselves, so I could share mine with my Teddy bear, which was a shiny light blue colour because when it needed a new covering that was the only material Muttie had for it.

In Vienna everything was different and exciting. We were staying in a hotel, which was really grand. We spent Christmas there, and Father Christmas gave me and Fred an electric railway set, which we set up in the hotel room. It was the first time we had ever been in a hotel. We were also eating in restaurants all the time, and sometimes we ate at the Automat cafes, where they have little rotating glass shelves where you can see all sorts of different open sandwiches with everything like salami and egg and rollmops on them. You just put some money in the slot and stop the shelves going round when you see the sandwich you want. Muttie let us operate the automat ourselves, which Fred and I really enjoyed doing.

In the daytime when Papa was working Mutti took us out to see Vienna. Once we even went to a cinema, the first time ever. They were showing a film about a plane crashing into the sea. As it was slowly sinking, Fred wet himself and had to be taken to the toilet. I think it must have been the sight of all that water. Then we saw a film with Shirley Temple, who is very pretty and just a little older than me, I think. She can sing and dance too and I fell in love with her. It lasted several years. Not the film, I mean.

Then we went to the City Hall Cellar restaurant in Vienna which is very famous. It had a lot of big glass tanks with fish swimming in them, and the waiter asked Papa to show him which ones we wanted to eat before fishing them out. I thought that was very cruel, but I did choose a fish and ate it after it was cooked. But I didn‘t watch the waiter fish it out.

Most weekends we went to visit new friends Papa had made at his office. Once we went to visit Herr. Moser and his wife who lived in Pressbaum, a village outside Vienna. There was a brook right outside their house and Fred and I were allowed to play in it. Frau Moser is very nice looking and has a smiley face. I like her a lot, but I still like Shirley Temple best. Herr Moser is serious looking, but he can make us all laugh because he can make a sound like a trumpet with his lips. He always does it to make me and Fred laugh.

Another time one of the men papa works with took us all out for a drive in his open sports car. That was the first time I ever had a ride in a car apart from the taxis we had to have in Vienna. Muttie had bought a special hat, it looked a bit like a flower pot upside down. It stayed on even when the car was driving quite fast.

After a few weeks at the hotel we moved into a flat in a house in a district of Vienna called Hietzing.. We lived upstairs and could look out across the road to the railway line that was used by the Orient Express. There was a little tunnel under the railway line that led to some fields and a small pond. Soon after we moved there, I was allowed to go for a walk on my own in the snow. I walked to the pond and on to the ice on it, then it broke and I fell in up to my knees. When I got back home I told Muttie I had slipped into a snow bank.

I was also given a scooter to play with, because although I was six years old I didn't go to kindergarten because I cried when I was left with a lot of children I didn't know. Fred already went to school and soon made some friends. One of them lived next door in a big house with a big garden. His father was an important Turkish government official. We sometimes played in their garden, and I could ride the friend's scooter which had a special pedal drive. He also had a cart with four wheels that you could sit in and move by pushing a handle bar backwards and forwards, and you could steer it with your feet.

When I got the scooter I was allowed to go and fetch the milk with it from the grocery shop around the corner. I liked the man there because at weekends he wore leather breeches and a jacket with big buttons made from deer antlers when he went out hunting with a big rifle he showed me.

I always went as fast as possible on my scooter, and once went around the corner too fast and crashed into the shopping basket an old lady was carrying. The milk bottle fell out of my basket and broke on the ground, and all the excitement made me wet myself as well, but otherwise I was OK and the old lady let me go without reporting me. I didn't tell Muttie I had wet myself, but she realised and made me change my trousers and underpants. After that I didn't go quite so fast on my scooter.

One afternoon our doorbell rang, and there stood a woman who lived next door. She told Muttie she had just seen a man take our washing off the clothes line, and when she asked him what he was doing he ran off and jumped over the fence. But he had dropped the washing, which was some sheets and shirts, on to the grass.

The woman said there had been quite a lot of thefts of washing in our area, and to be careful of what we hung up outside. Muttie was quite upset, because she felt really sorry for people who were so poor they had to steal washing.

Then we moved into a bigger flat in a house belonging to Frau Liebman, who lived in the flat above us with her daughter and her daughter's husband, a Jewish business man. One time Frau Liebmann asked us all for coffee when her son-in-law had just come back from Africa. He told us about going on safari and showed us a photograph of the lion he had shot. He also brought back a tropical helmet he had to wear there, and a shield and a spear which was used by the African natives. I thought he was really brave, and Papa later said he was surprised because he didn't think Jews liked doing that sort of travel. I can't remember us ever having known any Jews in Berlin.

Moedling

Now we have moved to Moedling, which is a small town right next to Vienna, so Papa can go there to his office by train every day. I am going to the elementary school called the Jakob Thoma school, and Fred is going to the Grammar school. Papa sometimes has to travel to places like Warsaw and Prague and Budapest on business. He takes his camera with him, so he can show us what these cities look like. He always wears a smart suit and a big hat, and sometimes he has a photo taken standing next to the people he does business with, and their wives too. I think Muttie feels a bit jealous, and she always dresses smartly when she goes out, much more so than she used to in Berlin.

Muttie does most of the housework, but she has Fraeulein Anna who lives in the basement of the house next door with her brother, to help her in the house. We have a large garden at the back of the house, with big walnut trees and an apricot tree. We live on the upper ground floor of the house which belongs to Fraeulein Tomanek, who has some rooms in the basement and a study on our floor, but she is not at the house very often because she is a student at Innsbruck University. Her father was a very important person in the government, and there is a big painting of her mother in a long dress in her study. Both her parents have died, so Fraeulein Tomanek is looked after by Herr Pawlitschek, who is called her guardian. She also has Fraeulein Anna to help her in the house when she is needed.

Fraeulein Anna used to be the servant of Fraeulein Tomanek's parents when they were alive. But now she only looks after the dog called Harry when Fraeulein Tomanek is not there. Harry now lives with us, and Fraeulein Anna comes over and feeds him twice a day. He is a very friendly type of Alsatian shepherd dog, but he frightens people who don't know him because he crinkles his nose and bares his teeth when he is pleased, like when he is about to get his bowl of food.

Herr Pablitschek is a nice friendly man who speaks with a strong Viennese accent. He is about as old as my father, perhaps a little older, and lives in a house next to the park in Moedling with his two sisters who have a tailoring business there. He has a small garage next to our veranda where he keeps an English BSA motorbike with a streamlined sidecar. This motorbike has very special instruments like the ones in cars, but they are on the handlebars. Herr Pablitschek is very proud of it and spends some time almost every weekend cleaning it and taking it out for rides. When Fraeulein Tomanek is staying at the house he takes her out for visits in it, with her sitting in the sidecar. I sometimes think he is in love with her, but I have never seen him kiss her. I don't think he is allowed to because he is her guardian, and he is much older.

On Sundays we go to the local swimming baths which have an indoor pool with showers and a large outdoor pool which also has an area which is used as an ice skating rink in the winter. After swimming we usually go to a restaurant called Fasching for our Sunday dinner. Last time we went Papa ordered breaded roast chicken. When it was put on the table we were all surprised. It still had the head with the comb on it and was all covered in breadcrumbs, even the head. We didn't really like that, so Papa didn't order it again after that.

Now I am lying on a blanket in the garden reading a book about Old Shatterhand, which is the name given him by the Apache Indians, because he can knock people out with a single blow to the side of the head. He is studying their culture by living amongst them, but now he has to fight a duel with Winnetou, the son of the Indian chief. The duel has to take place under the water of the Silver Lake, and I can't wait to read what happens.

But now Harry comes along and licks my face. Then I hear the bell from the front gate, and Muttie calls me to let in Gert Heidermann, my German friend who lives the other side of Moedling. We talk about Old Shatterhand and Winnetou and then Muttie gives us cocoa and bread and dripping for our afternoon snack. After that Gert starts to wrestle with me, which he likes to do a lot. He is a little bigger than I am, but I manage to get him on his back very quickly. Then he wants to start again, so we have another go, and he is on his back again very soon. Then we set up the electric railway in the garden, and by the time we have finished, it's time for him to go home. I am glad we didn't have another wrestle because I don't really like wrestling. .

Now it's seven o'clock and I take my scooter to meet Papa at the station. He looks very grand in his business suit and a hat with a stiff brim. He always carries an umbrella, and he uses it to push my scooter along while I am standing on it. When we meet anybody we know they greet Papa respectfully because they know he is English.

I was born in Berlin and have never been to England, where Papa was born. He has spent a lot of time in Berlin where he met Muttie before they were married. Muttie has never been to England and doesn't understand English, so we speak only German together.

When we get home Muttie gives Papa his evening meal. We will have had sandwiches for our supper, but Papa always has a cooked meal because he does not have a midday meal at the office. I sometimes sit at the table and listen to Papa and Muttie talking. Fred will be doing some homework which he should do in the afternoon, but he often goes to visit friends instead. After his meal, Papa puts on his smoking jacket and either reads the paper or plays the piano, and it's usually a piece he calls Liszt's Hungarian Rhapsody, which he always practises.

Sometimes in the winter Fred and I can go to the butcher in town who makes hot black pudding and sauerkraut that we can bring home in special pots with lids and handles for carrying. On the way there we have to go past the weir in the Moedling stream, and after that past where our shoemaker lives. He is a bent old man with a beard, and we can see him working in his workshop even in the evening when we go past. He has a lot of children in his house, and I think they are really poor. On the way back Fred swings his full pot right over his head. I think he just likes to show off.

After our evening meal Fred and I go to bed. Our bedroom is a large room next to our parent's bedroom, and has a door leading to the veranda, one to Papa and Muttie's bedroom, and another one to the entrance hall. There is also a small door opening on to a little room with the iron stove for heating the flat in the winter. Muttie has to carry the coal and the wood to keep the stove going in the winter. Even then it sometimes gets very cold by the morning, and the double windows have ice on the inside when we get up.

In the winter months we can hear the music from the loudspeaker at the ice rink In the evenings. They always play the same waltzes over and over again, so both Fred and I can whistle all of them.

At School

Now it's winter and I am at school. Herr Gruber, our class teacher, is a very quiet man and never raises his voice. I sit next to Sepp

Hirtl who is taller than me but isn't so good at arithmetic. We have to copy the sums Herr Gruber is writing on the blackboard into our exercise books for our homework. After the break, when we can run around in the big school yard and play catch with our friends, we are doing writing and spelling. Today the local priest is taking religion, but since I am not a Catholic I am allowed to go home together with my friend Herbert Krisch and about six others who are Protestant or Jewish. But we will have to go to a separate religion lesson in the afternoon.

Herbert lives next door to the Protestant Church in the Scheffergasse. He can even hear pastor Mueller practising on the church organ. The religion class Herbert and I and the other Protestants go to is at a little house in the Pfarrgasse not very far from the Town Hall in Moedling. Pastor Mueller is a big man and he usually wears a bigger hat than Papa's when he goes out. He has a high forehead and a lot of hair on top of his head, not like the Catholic priest who is really a monk and is bald on top but has a lot of hair around the sides of his head.

Pastor Mueller tells us about Jesus and how we should think about poor children who don't get enough to eat or go around in ragged clothes without shoes. Some children in our class are poor, but they all wear shoes. Some can't afford to wear knickerbockers in the winter which are warmer than leather shorts. I feel sorry for them but I can't do anything about it. I know Papa and Muttie wouldn't allow me to give them my knickerbockers because then I would have to wear shorts instead.

We all carry satchels to school for our exercise books and homework. I and some other boys also bring bread rolls to eat at break time, which lasts about twenty minutes. We can run and play in the school yard or eat our rolls. When it's raining or cold in the winter, we can stay inside in the school hall. There is always a teacher keeping an eye on us to make sure we are behaving properly and not fighting or bullying each other. Some of the poorer children are sometimes bullied and called 'Sozis' because they come from families who are unemployed or doing factory work and usually belong to a union which means they support the Socialist party in Austria. The teachers are mostly

Catholics, and I know Herr Gruber is because I have seen him go to the St Othmar church, which is the Catholic church up the hill from the Town Hall.

I have another friend in the same class called Walter Kainrath. Walter lives in a flat which is a part of the swimming pool building. His father is an engineer and he looks after all the machinery for heating the indoor and the outdoor pools, and also the ice factory, the skating rink and the laundry, which all belong to the swimming pool. He makes Walter stay home in the afternoons to do all his homework, and I think Walter takes longer to do his than I do, so I don't often see him apart from school. But sometimes after the open air pool closes I can see Walter swimming on his own from the indoor pool. He is a very good swimmer and does the freestyle. He glides through the water like a fish. The only time he is not allowed to swim after closing time is when Herr Eichert, the swimming pool guard and swimming instructor, has a training session with Count von so-an-so (I don't know his name) who sometimes comes in a big Tatra car which has its engine at the back.

1932

At home

Today I've got to stay at home in bed because I've got ear ache. I had it about three months ago, and now Muttie has called in Dr Loewe again. He is a short man with a moustache and a small beard and has glasses clipped to his nose. Muttie said he is Jewish but she has been told by friends that he is very good. He says I've got middle ear inflammation and have to have bed rest and regular drips of warm oil into the ears. So it's come back again and it's very painful. Dr Loewe said I must stay in bed until he says I can get up. During the day I can be in Papa and Muttie's bed because it is more comfortable, and easier for Dr Loewe to examine me.

After a week in bed I am getting better, and Dr.Loewe doesn't have to come back. But he said I should have ultra-violet treatment at his surgery in the Elizabethstrasse for a few weeks. So when

I am well enough to go out, Muttie takes me there, and Dr Loewe makes me undress down to my underpants and gives me some coloured goggles to wear when I get on to the bed underneath the big Ultra-violet lamp. I have to stay there for about fifteen minutes. It is supposed to be the same as being out in the sun, but of course outside it's still winter.

After a few weeks I can stop the treatment, but Dr Loewe said I should have a rest after lunch for about an hour every day. When I do this I get very bored, but I am allowed to read if I can't sleep. I got hold of a Catholic Church booklet about children and dogs which has a lot of stories about how Jesus wants us to be good to animals, and this is what I read before I fall asleep.

After what Pastor Mueller has been telling us about Jesus, and reading about what Jesus wants us to do, I think I really want to be good and do everything he tells us. I will try to go to Church on Sundays more often, but it is difficult because most of the time we go swimming then with Muttie and Papa. But I have decided to follow Jesus and set an example to all my friends. I don't tell Muttie and Papa about it, because they never talk about Jesus and they never go to Church, so I am afraid they wouldn't understand.

Every morning of the week except Sundays I go to the Jakob Thoma school. I carry my satchel with exercise books and bread rolls for break time. Fred goes to the Grammar school which starts at a different time, so we don't go together. Sometimes I meet some of my class mates on the way to school and we walk along together. I have made friends with one boy who looks a bit different and some of the others make fun of him because he has a big head. He doesn't say a lot, so I can do most of the talking. He is called Hansl. In March I am allowed to go for a walk into the Anninger Woods with him. There is still a lot of snow around, and the sun is shining. I lead the way up the Anninger hill telling Hansl about Winnetou and Old Shatterhand, but then when the sunset made the snow look pink Hansl began to say we should go back. When we got back to my house it was getting dark, and Muttie was angry with me. She told Hansl to hurry back home, because his mother had telephoned her and she was going to tell the police we were missing. After that Hansl wasn't allowed to go out with me again.

Uncle Paul and aunt Hertha

Uncle Paul and aunt Hertha have come from Berlin to stay with us for a week. Fraeulein Tomanek has let them use the room she uses as her study on our floor as a bedroom. Uncle Paul is full of fun and really enjoying himself. Aunt Herta is a little shy, but she is very friendly and likes to talk and play with me, perhaps because they don't have children. When I went to stay with them in Berlin with Muttie last Christmas, Uncle Paul dressed up as father Xmas and brought me some presents in a sack. I never told him that I knew it was him all the time. Aunt Herta made sure I got pork crackling to eat when we were staying with them, because Muttie had told her I really like it. Every time I went to bed they had hidden another little toy car under my pillow, so I was always quite keen to go to bed at night.

While they are staying with us Papa has taken time off from work, so we all spend a lot of time in the garden, and we have been in the Vienna woods a couple of times with them. In the evenings they play cards, and sometimes chess, which uncle Paul plays with Papa. Uncle Paul is a policeman in Berlin, and we know he is a Sozi, that's what we call the Socialists. I don't think he gets on very well with his brother, my uncle Walter, who has a business selling batteries. I have heard Muttie say it's because uncle Walter doesn't like the Sozis, because he thinks they are not very different from Communists.

Uncle Paul has brought me a book from Berlin called 'Emil and the Detectives'. It's about a thief who cheats people, and how Emil and his friends form a gang called 'the detectives' to trap him. It's really quite exciting, and it all happens in Berlin where I come from. Emil also has a girl in his gang, and she actually owns a bicycle and helps to chase the thief on it. They are all praised by the Police when they have helped capture the thief, and Emil is very proud of his detectives. I think next time I have friends come to visit we'll play at being detectives, and I will be Emil because I know Berlin.

After Uncle Paul and Auntie Hertha had gone back to Berlin, Papa and Muttie gave me a big book called Tom Sawyer and Huckleberry Finn. It's by an American writer, and it's really funny in places, like where Tom makes out to his friend what fun it is to paint his auntie's fence, and then leaves him to finish the job. Later on in the book it gets quite exciting when they are looking for an Indian who is hiding in a cave because he has committed a crime. Tom also has a girl friend called Becky. I think he will probably marry her when he grows up. Huckleberry Finn also helps a negro slave escape, so I think they are really very adventurous.

1933

Where babies come from.

This afternoon I am going to the weekly religion lesson with Pastor Mueller. It is held in an upstairs room of an old house that belongs to the Moedling council. They have put some desks in it, and since there are only fourteen of us the little room is big enough. Of course the Catholics are able to use the Jacob Thoma School for their religion lessons because there are a lot more Catholics than Protestants in Austria.

Pastor Mueller is quite cheerful today. He reads from a bible story and he stops when he gets to the word 'begat'. Then he says for all of us who know where babies come from to put up our hands. We all put up our hands, but I don't really know for sure. I do know they are not brought by a stork, and I think they come out of a woman's belly buttons, or perhaps even from their backsides, a bit like going to the toilet.

Then Pastor Mueller says to put up our hands again if our parents told us. Only three put up their hands. So he says to put up our hands if we learnt it from friends, and all bar two of the rest put up their hands, Then Pastor Mueller turns to the two of us who haven't put up our hands yet and asks how we found out. The other boy says he found out from a book, so when Pastor Mueller turns to me I lie and say so did I. But I go red in the face and I don't think he believes me, but he just smiles and we go on with the bible reading.

Afterwards I am really worried that I still don't really know. I don't like to ask Papa and Muttie, particularly Muttie because she doesn't like me to look at the medical book that shows you women's female parts, and I feel too embarrassed to ask Fred and show him how little I know, because I am sure he does. He often goes to visit a friend down the road who knows what the courting couples do in the woods together, because he stalks them and watches them, so he probably also knows where babies come from. And I am too embarrassed to ask any of my friends because I don't want to let on how ignorant I am.

Some time after this, I am alone in our house one morning when Muttie has gone to visit Frau Hobiger. I go to the sideboard where the large books are kept, and I look at the medical dictionary. Then I look under 'birth', and there is a section through a woman's body showing the baby, and from this I can see that the only way the baby can come out is from between the woman's legs. Just then Muttie comes home earlier then I thought, and when she sees me looking at the pictures in the medical dictionary, she takes the book away saying 'You don't need to know about these things. It's far better for you to be playing in the garden on a fine day like this'.

Girls are very interesting to me, and I always wonder how they can pee. In the entrance hall of the Moedling indoor swimming pool there is a large painting on the wall with a nude lady on it, and she has what looks like a black triangle between her legs. Every time I go swimming and there in no one else in the entrance hall, I have a look at the black triangle, but there is nothing more to see

Not long ago we got some new neighbours in the house opposite, and Muttie let me ask their little girl over to play. We soon got bored, because she wasn't interested in Old Shatterhand or Winnetou or Emil and the Detectives. Then I got this idea she might be willing to show me how girls pee, and I asked her whether she would show me hers if I showed her mine. She was quite willing to do it, and was just pulling down her knickers on the veranda of the garden shed when Muttie called out from the house. She called 'Eddie, what are you two doing there?' I just went red in the face and said nothing. Then Muttie said 'Its time for your lunch, Lottie, your mother will be waiting for you.'

But I still don't know what starts babies off, and what makes women have them. I think it's got something to do with what Fred's friend spies on courting couples for. Also, I have read in the 'Arabian Nights' stories about men and women sleeping together, and I think this has something to do with starting babies. It doesn't even tell you about that in the medical book we have. One good person to ask would be Pastor Mueller himself, because his wife has babies quite often, she has had three already. But of course I would never ask him, because then all my friends would know that I didn't know.

I could ask Muttie or Papa, but I feel ashamed to. And I'm sure Muttie think's it's something you shouldn't know about until you are old enough to get married. I am sure Fred knows.

A walk in the Vienna Woods.

Today we are walking up past the quarry into the woods going up to the Anninger hill. It's Papa, Muttie, me and Harry, and Herr and Frau Hobiger with Trudl, their daughter. Muttie and Papa got to know the Hobigers through the German Expatriate Association called 'The Bund', a sort of club for Germans living in Austria, but the Hobigers actually came from Rumania. Herr Hobiger is wearing dark trousers and a white shirt open at the neck, with sleeves rolled up. Frau Hobiger, Muttie and Trudl are all wearing dirndls, which are like dresses with a belt and cut away around the bosoms but with a blouse underneath.

Papa has his knickerbockers on that he always wears now when he is at home and not going to the office.. He didn't have knickerbockers in Berlin because we didn't do a lot of walking there. I wear leather shorts now except in the winter, when I wear knickerbockers like Papa. I also have a little botanical drum hung round my neck. It's like a metal box with a lid, which I can use to put in any unusual plants we might find, but I also use it for some bread rolls with Schnitzel in them which Muttie has made for us.

The grownups are talking about Herr Hobiger's problems at the bank where he works. It's to do with his boss, the bank manager, who is a Jew. Herr Hobiger doesn't like Jews anyway, so maybe that is why he is a Nazi. When he wears his suit for the office, he has a Swastika badge pinned on underneath his coat lapel, so other people can't see it unless he shows it to them. But I don't think he would show it to his boss.

Trudl is about two years older than me, and quite a bit taller. She is quite good looking, and she goes to the girls' Grammar school. She is telling me a story she has read in a book about a girl who goes into the woods with her boyfriend, who asks her to play cowboys and Indians with her. Part of this game consists of the girl agreeing to let him tie her to a tree. But I don't think she really read this, because it wasn't very long ago she told me about dreaming she was being tied to a tree. I just think she has a thing about being tied up. So I start changing the conversation to talk about Winnetou and old Shatterhand. Then Trudl gets bored and runs after Harry and throws a stick for him to fetch. When we get to the Richardshof, which is a restaurant where you can also sit in the open on benches with tables, all the grownups order beer, and Trudl and I are given lemonade. Then we take out our Schnitzel rolls. This is what I enjoy most on our walks.

There are a lot of people at the restaurant. Some have come from Vienna, and a lot of the men are wearing leather shorts and mountain boots and some even have Tyrolean hats with a feather stuck on, lik the hunters who go deer shooting in the autumn. We secretly laugh at them, because they are just townies and not really out-door people like us who live close to the woods and often walk there.

Later on, when we are back home, the Hobiger's have coffee with us because we live on the way back to their house. I show Trudl the baby ducklings Papa has given me to play with. We have a little pond in the garden with a model sailing boat on it, and the little ducks like to swim around the boat. It looks quite funny. Trudl picks up one of the ducklings and strokes it, but it soon jumps out of her hands. Trudl doesn't have any pets at her home, because they don't have room for them.

Papa likes giving us presents at Easter time. This Easter he gave me a big cardboard egg. When I opened it up, it had a white fluffy guinea pig inside. I was really amazed and excited. I called him Peter, he has his own little wooden box with straw in it in our bedroom now, and when I am there he can run around the room. He makes little squeaking noises when he is hungry, which is quite often. Sometimes I let him run out in the garden, but I have to keep an eye on him so he doesn't get out into the neighbours' gardens. We had a tortoise once which we used to let out in the garden, but one time, after we had it for a year, we didn't keep our eyes on it and it disappeared.

Christmas

Every Christmas Eve Fred and I have to dress up in our best clothes, and then, before the evening meal, we each have to stand by the Christmas tree and say a poem that we learnt by heart, first Fred and then me. Then Papa and Muttie give us our presents. This time I got a big book called 'the New Universum' which has a lot in it about adventures and technical things like sports cars which Papa and Muttie know I like, and I asked them to tell Father Christmas. I also got another Meccano set to add to the one I already have. Fred got an air rifle which has a chromium plated barrel and fires bullets with a little fluffy tail when it's loaded. It's very clever, and I am already thinking to learn how to shoot it when Fred is not using it. I can imagine myself as a hunter in the Wild West, a bit like Old Shatterhand, though he didn't actually do any hunting.

After we got our presents Papa put on some Christmas records on our gramophone which has a very big loudspeaker like the ones they have in cinemas, because Papa's firm hire them out to cinemas and let him have this one. It makes a very good quality of sound, and can be made very loud too. Then we have my favourite roast goose for supper, and both Papa and Muttie have some very good white wine to drink, and Fred and I have lemonade.

Last weekend I had to play a shepherd in the Jesus nativity play in our Protestant church, because Pastor Mueller said this is what we should do if we believe in Jesus. When I told Papa and Muttie they said I could take part in the play, and they came and watched me kneeling in front of the crib in the play, although they don't normally go to church. After the play pastor Mueller thanked us all for taking part, and he also spoke to some of the parents, including Papa and Muttie. I think he wants them to come to Church more often. Papa congratulated Pastor Mueller on the performance we all put up. Then I had to go to get out of the smock I was wearing and we all went home.

On New Year's Eve this year Muttie and Papa are going out to a local club for music and dancing. They are going with the Hobigers, because they have become good friends with them The Hobigers sometimes come to us to play bridge in the evening, and I think it's quite a serious game. I don't think Frau Hobiger, who is called Christl by her friends, takes it very seriously though, and very often she holds up the game to have an argument with Herr Hobiger, who is called Fritz. But it usually ends with them all just having a big laugh, and they also drink a lot of wine when they are playing.

1934

The Party

It's February and the weather is quite mild. Papa is having a party. He has invited the Earlys, the Mosers, the Winklers and the Findlayson.

The Mosers arrive first, and I go to the garden gate to let them in. Herr Moser starts making his trumpet sound when he sees me coming. He is really funny and I am laughing and so is Frau Moser. Just then we hear a noise like thunder coming from the direction of Vienna. We stop talking and listen. Then it happens again, but it's February and there are no thunder clouds. Then Papa and Muttie come out to listen as well. Papa says he heard on the news that the Army has surrounded the Karl Marx court in Vienna, which is a block of flats built for workers. He thinks they must be firing their cannons at the flats. We keep hearing the thunder, but after a while we all go inside.

Then the Winklers arrive. The Winklers have come from Germany and Herr Winkler has only just started work at Papa's company. He lost one leg in the war, so he has an artificial leg and walks with a stick. He has curly brown hair and a round, cheerful face. Mrs Winkler is nice looking and has black hair, but she doesn't laugh much, particularly not at Herr Winkler's jokes. They are all talking together about what's happening in Vienna when the next guests arrive. They are the Findlaysons. Mr Findlayson is a Scottish teacher who teaches English at an international school in Vienna, and she is an Austrian Jewish woman. They have only been married for a little while, and they live in a flat along the Schillerstrasse down near the railway station. Muttie says she has a very Jewish looking face. I think she must be very clever, and Papa says she can speak English very well. It's just a pity she has such a Jewish looking nose...

The last guests are the Earleys. They are a Scottish couple who live not far from us in Moedling. They are very nice, and they have a shoe shop in Vienna where they sell English shoes to important people who can afford them, like barons and people who have a 'von' in front of their name. Mr Earley has a high forehead and not much hair. He speaks in a croaky voice and chuckles after he has finished saying anything, even when it isn't funny. Mrs Earley has white hair and round cheeks and smiles a lot. They have a woman servant called Gertie who lives in their house with them, Their children are already quite old, older than Fred even, and except at holiday times they live away from their parents in England. Their younger son is called Boysie. He goes to a famous military school called Sandhurst, and comes to stay with his parents in his school holidays. His brother and three sisters are all older than him but they also sometimes come to stay with their parents.

While the grownups are talking together over a glass of wine in the dining room, Fred and his friend Peppi are preparing to give a Punch and Judy show in the children's room, which is what we call Fred's and my bedroom. Fred has said I can do a turn beforehand to show off my headstand. After we have brought in the chairs, we ring a bell and the visitors come in and sit down on the row of chairs in front of the Punch and Judy theatre.

Then Fred announces that before they start the Punch and Judy show, I will demonstrate my famous headstand. I put a cushion on the floor and bend down to put my head on it, then I kick my legs upwards and manage to balance on my head, supporting myself with my arms. Everybody is quiet and impressed. Then when I start to do a forward roll, I let go a little fart. There is a silence, and I get up with a red face and say that wasn't actually meant to be part of the act. Then Papa laughs and soon they are all laughing, and then they clap and I have to bow.

When Fred and Peppy start their Punch and Judy, everybody is in a good mood, and they also laugh at the stunts by Punch and Judy and the policeman and the devil. Fred and Peppy make their voices quite deep and like grown ups, but now and again they forget and when the devil who is meant to be very fierce speaks in Fred's normal voice and everybody is laughing again. At the end they all clap and go into the dining room where Muttie has laid out a cold buffet supper, and Fred, Peppi and I stay together and have our supper in the playroom. After Peppi has gone home, we say good night to everybody. The thunder of the canons stopped some time ago, although we didn't know when.

The next day we heard it was all because the Sozis had tried to overthrow the government. It was the first time I heard about Socialists being so strong as to try to do such a thing, because they were mostly the poor and the unemployed. But they didn't win, and later on the Chancellor who is called Dollfuss, made sure that they were punished. He even had some of them hanged, and after that the Socialist Party in Austria was banned.

Climbing the Rax

This year for our summer holiday Papa is taking us to Semmering. We are staying in a hotel there, and Fred and I share a room. Every day we go for long walks through the forest. Papa, Fred and I have rucksacks to carry drinks and bread rolls for our lunch. Papa always wears his plus-fours and sometimes a flat cap, and carries a map. One day he tells us we are going to climb the Rax, a really big mountain near the Hotel. It's 2000 metres high, and I can't believe that we will get to the top. We go some of the way by bus, and then we go on some steep paths through woods until we reach a path that goes up through some rocks.

Then we have to hold on to steel ropes fastened to the rocks along the side of the path, and sometimes we have to pull ourselves up along these ropes to help us climb. Papa says we shouldn't look back down in case we get dizzy, only forward. At one point though we can't help looking down over the rocks along the path, and it's really frightening. You can see practically over all of Lower Austria, and if you look down you can see where we started from a long way below us. Then we reach the top of the Rax, and suddenly we are on a flat meadow with some flowers, even some Edelweiss, and there is a Gasthof not very far ahead. This is the best part of mountain climbing, when we can sit at the table and have our lemonade and Salami rolls, and Papa and Muttie have beers to make up for our hard work to get there. Then we go to the viewpoints and look out over the countryside and the other mountains all around.

Getting down again is even more frightening, but Papa says with all the steel ropes it is quite safe as long as we keep to the path. When we get back to the hotel, we are all tired and have a sleep.

Most evenings I play with a little matchbox Meccano set, when I am not in the Hotel playroom with Fred and some other children. Once we played doctors and nurses there, and I think Fred likes to examine some of the girls his own age there, just to make sure there is nothing wrong with them.

At the brick ponds

Today Papa, Muttie, Fred and I went to the brick ponds for a swim in the evening. They are where they used to mine the clay for bricks, close to the Trieste highway and about twenty minutes' walk from Moedling. It's still very hot, even though it's after six o'clock. The pond beach is quite sandy, but not very flat, and you must be able to swim if you go there. Even so, there have been stories in the newspapers about people drowning, so we are always careful.

I learnt to swim at the Moedling open air swimming pool, and I taught myself, even though I was only seven years old. Here at the Brick Ponds there are no changing cabins, and you can swim for free. We all undress, us boys using a towel draped around us, and Muttie and Papa have a proper changing robe. We are all hot and sweating when we go into the water, which is quite warm but still very refreshing. We are close to a steep drop down to the water, where they have put a diving board, which is really just a long wooden plank.

When we come out of the water and start drying ourselves, we hear the noise of a motor cycle, and it is the Koch family on a very old-fashioned motor bicycle with a side-car. We first met the Kochs at the German Expatriate Association meeting. Herr Koch is a sales representative for a German company, and he lives with his family in a semi-basement flat in the next town to Moedling. He is a thin man with a bald head and he is always doing funny things. His wife is very round in comparison, and has a big bust as well. Their two daughters are very similar to the mother, but not quite so round, and they share the seat in the sidecar. They are older than Fred even, and always giggling at something, and I feel shy with them. But really they take little notice of anybody else, particularly when their father is with them, because he always gives them something to laugh at.

The Kochs don't have changing robes, and they change behind the motor bike. The mother and the girls all have very tight swimsuits, which makes them quite interesting to look at. But I try not to, in case they notice I am staring at them, which would make me go red in the face. As soon as he has gotten into his old-fashioned full length black swim suit, Herr Koch gets on to the spring board and bows to the right and left. Then he makes a couple of runs but doesn't jump. Then he stands at the end of the board and stretches out his arms like a champion diver, and looks as though he is concentrating. Then he changes his mind and goes back towards his giggling family. Finally he takes a run and dives in, making a big belly flop with his arms outstretched. Everybody is laughing and applauding, so he comes out of the water and does a repeat performance. His wife is smiling all the time, and the girls never stop giggling. But I don't think they are embarrassed by their father, they are probably used to him being the centre of attention.

Before it gets dark we get dressed to go home. We leave before the Kochs, since we have to walk. Sometime later they pass us on their motorbike with a great deal of hooting and giggling and shouting. Soon the full moon helps to light our way, and lots of glow worms as well. Although it is still very warm, we have to keep covered up because of the mosquitoes. When we get home, Harry welcomes us with a lot of tooth fletching and snorting. We are all very tired, and Fred and I go to bed right away.

At the swimming pool

We go to the Moedling Town Baths with the indoor and oputdoor swimming pools quite often. There is also an ice factory attached, where they make big chunks of ice for people who have an ice box to keep their food in, as we have. My friend Herbert Krisch's father is the financial manager, and my friend Walter Kainrath's father is the Engineering manager. He has to be at the baths most of the time, and that is why they live in a flat which is attached to the swimming pool buildings. Sometimes when we are at the indoor pool, we see Herr Krisch looking down at us from the gallery when he is walking between the offfices which are up there. We also sometimes see Herr Kainrath there, and he gives us a wave because he knows me. Herr Krisch comes under the director of the swimming baths, and Herr Kainrath as well.

One time when I came to play with Walter at their flat, he took me down into the engine room for the pools. We met his father there and he explained all about this huge engine they have there to drive all the equipment they need for heating the pool and providing steam for the laundry attached to the pool, and also for making the ice for the ice boxes and freezing the ice for the skating rink in the winter. I think Herr Kainrath is a very important man for the Town Baths, because he does most of the work and only has one or two assistants. I think he is quite strict with Walter, who is never allowed to come out to play until he has done all his homework. But he also gives him a reward when he works well, because last Easter Walter got a bicycle as a present. But he is only allowed to ride it if his father or mother are there to keep an eye on him.

Today I'm at the open air swimming pool together with Fred. Muttie and Papa have gone on holiday on their own to Yugoslavia, and have left Fraeulein Anna to look after us. It's twelve o'clock and already very hot. I'm sitting on a wooden bunk bed with a towel over my shoulders to stop me getting sunburnt, and reading a book about some adventures in the jungles of Borneo when I'm not watching what is going on around me.

Fred is playing ping-pong with one of his friends. They are both wearing the EWASC swimming trunks to show they belong to the swimming club, which is very famous in Austria. EWASC is short for 'First Viennese Amateur Swimming Club'.

On the roof of the changing room building I can sometimes see the heads of the naked sunbathers. On one side of the clock tower it's for men and on the other for women. I can't understand why they aren't ashamed to show themselves without anything on. I wonder if there are many like the nude woman in the painting in the indoor pool with the black triangle.

On the next bunk but one I have been watching a young man and a girl with a big bosom. They've been talking together for some time, then she goes off to one of the rented changing cabins on the terrace where the childrens' sandpit is. After a little while the man went into the same cabin, and they haven't yet come out, even after half an hour. Perhaps they're kissing and making love, which I don't know what it means exactly, though I believe I am in love with Shirley Temple.

I also like Erica who is the sister of Ilse, the sister of one of Fred's boyfriends. I sometimes see Ilse on my way to school, because she goes to the Gymnasium for girls which is on my way to my school. She is always laughing or giggling together with her school friends, and never takes any notice of me, which is good because I always go red in the face when I think she might look at me, I don't know why. Perhaps I think how embarrassed I would be if she found out I thought she was really good looking. Anyway, I still like Shirley Temple best...

This evening Fraulein Anna is giving us a Goulash for our evening meal. Afterwards Fred is allowed to go visit his friend Peppi who lives just the other side of the Town Baths. Then Anna and a woman from down the road take Harry out for a walk, and I am allowed to come along. They both talk a lot together, and I soon get bored, because it's mainly about what some of the people in the road where we live do. They are talking about Herr Court Counsellor Sommerfeld, who lives next door but one from us. He and his wife often take their big collie dog for a walk. Herr Sommerfeld is bald and has a beard. He has glasses clipped to his nose that make his eyes look large and fierce, and he wears breeches held up not with a belt but something like a black shawl around his middle. Frau Sommerfeld always walks behind him, and they never speak to anyone else they meet in our road. I think it is because they are very important, and can only talk to other people who are also important. Fraeulein Anna is saying that the Court Councillor's housekeeper, who lives in their house, has told her that she is only allowed free time on Sundays, and she has to do all the cleaning and the cooking and laundry, and that Frau Sommerfeld doesn't do anything but look after her dresses and Herr Sommerfeld's clothes.

When we get to the fields at the end of our road, I can let Harry run off the lead, which he really enjoys. He goes chasing after rabbits, but most of the time he just likes sniffing at what other dogs have left behind, and then he leaves his own for other dogs to sniff.

When we get back home Fraeulein Anna lets me listen to the radio. This evening they are broadcasting an operetta called the Czardas Princess. It's all about a gypsy singer who falls in love with a prince. I think she must be very beautiful, and I imagine what I would do if I were the prince. Then Fred comes home and we go to bed. Fred has a reading light over his bed and is allowed to read until nine o'clock. I am always asleep before he is.

Dollfuss is murdered

Yesterday we heard on the radio that Chancellor Dollfuss had been shot and killed in his office in the Chancellery. We all think it must have been the Socialists, because Dollfuss was the one who ordered the Karl Marx workers flats to be fired on in February and then had some of the workers hanged. But it turns out it was a group of Nazis disguised as Austrian Army soldiers who got into the Chancellery. Another group got into the Vienna broadcasting station and had them announced that Dollfuss had resigned and that his place would be taken by a well-known Nazi.

But by then the Chancellery was surrounded by the police and army, and they negotiated with the Nazis and in the end allowed them to march out. Everybody is asking why they were allowed to get away with murder. Later we were told that Schuschnigg, one of the Dollfuss government ministers, would become Chancellor.

Herr Meyer, our class teacher, looked very serious at the beginning of class the day after the murder. I think he is really a 'black', because he is Catholic and goes to Church every Sunday, and he was probably a Dollfuss supporter. I think it's a shame, because I really like him, he is just very old-fashioned in everything. Also, I can't understand how anyone can go along with all that incense and drinking wine at communion.

This evening the Hobigers were here again, and I was sitting on the sofa reading a book whilst they were playing bridge with Muttie and Papa. Then later when they were having coffee Herr Hobiger was saying that he thought that Dollfuss, although he was only a little man, was really a Catholic Fascist more like Mussolini, and he doesn't think it was really Nazis that shot him but the Communists.

Then he talked about when he was shot in the war, and how he was hit by a bullet from the side that went right through him. I know, because I have seen him at the swimming pool, and you can see he has a scar on each side. Then Papa told them about some of his own experiences in the war. He was in the German army stationed on the Eastern front fighting against the Russians. One evening he was on guard in the trenches, and he saw some lights flashing alongside the woods further along, so he called out 'who goes there', but the lights just kept on flashing. So he called out again, and then realised that the lights were just something natural that comes from rotten tree trunks. I think it's called St. Vitus dance.

Then Papa talks about how he was transferred back behind the front to help in finding out things from the British prisoners of war in a camp there. He had to dress up in the uniform of the British pilots who had been captured, and they put him amongst the prisoners to pose as one of them, to try and find out information about what their planes were like and how many they had. He said he never found out very much, but he showed the Hobigers some photos of himself in a British pilots' uniform which were taken by one of his comrades at the time.

1935

Skating in Laxenburg.

Now it's winter and we sometimes go skating on a Sunday morning with Muttie and Papa at the Moedling ice rink next to the open air swimming pool. They are skating in a separate part of the rink roped off from the main part for skaters learning to dance on the ice. Fred and I are going around with the rest of the skaters and sometimes stop and watch Papa and Muttie at their lesson. We just learnt skating ourselves, and we can now skate quite well and don't fall over very often. Fred has proper ice skating boots with the skates screwed on to the boots. My skates are called 'clamp steamers' because they are clamped on my ordinary walking boots. I can skate quite fast on them, almost as fast as Fred, without falling over. But a lot of the skaters are still learners, and they often fall over and slide along the ice.

Today Papa has organised a skating party for us together with Fraeulein Tomanek and Herr Pablitscheck. It's Sunday, and we all get on a bus to Laxenburg. In the Laxenburg park, which is alongside where the Emperor Franz Joseph had his summer residence, there is a lake with an island which has an old castle on it called the Franzenburg. We have to walk from the bus stop to the lake carrying our skates, and Papa also carries a gramophone so they can dance to the music.

The lake is frozen solid because it has been quite cold. We all have pullovers on, and the grownups have coats with fur collars. They start skating to the music, and Fred and I are surprised to see how well Fraeulein Tomanek and Herr Pablitschek can waltz on the ice, better than Papa and Muttie who are still learning. There are a few other skaters here, quite different from being on the ice rink in Moedling. Muttie says it's really romantic to skate to the Vienna waltzes right next to the old castle on the island. Fred and I pretend we have partners and try to skate to the music like the grownups, but we feel silly and burst out loughing. Papa has asked me to wind up the gramophone when it starts to run down, so I feel quite important.

After an hour on the lake it's getting dark and we pack our things and walk through the park to catch the bus back. It's been really exciting to skate on the frozen lake, and I think Fraeulein Tomanek and Herr Pablitschek enjoyed themselves as much as we did. When we get home Muttie gives us Frankfurters with potato salad, and the grownups drink a glass of wine with their meal. It's the best skating I have done, and we are all looking forward to the next time.

I am arrested!

Wolfgang Winkler and I are at the stone quarry. Wolfgang is at the same school with me, but in a different class. We have been for a walk, it's a sunny day, and I tell Wolfgang about the adventures of Tom Sawyer and Huckleberry Finn. We think of ourselves as being like them, and are looking for an adventure ourselves. We are on a bridle way looking down the steep slope to the café below.

Wolfgang picks up a stone the size of an orange and throws it towards the corrugated iron roof of the café. It falls just short of the roof on to the hillside. So I have a go, and mine falls short too. So we start a competition who can hit the roof. Eventually Wolfgang gets to hit the roof, so I have a really big try, and I manage to hit it as well.

Just then the owner of the café comes running out. He looks all round him into the sky, and then sees us. 'You lousy rascals', he shouts, 'you come down here at once or I'll have the police on you'. Now we're both frightened. There's only one quick way back into the town, and that's past the café. Wolfgang says 'come on, we'll go back home the long way, round the back of the hill'. He starts running, but I'm undecided. The man is still shouting 'you come down here now, both of you, I'm phoning the police now.'

Wolfgang runs up the hill and soon I can't see him anymore. I am thinking I had better go down. But I am still undecided whether I should give myself up. When I get on to the main track that goes past the café, I hide behind some bushes, and I can see Fred coming up towards me. He is bringing a rucksack with some bread rolls for me and Wolfgang, because Muttie had said we could stay and have our lunch in the woods, and Fred would bring it in a rucksack because he was visiting a friend not far from where we were. As he is walking past the café, the owner comes out and speaks to him. They both look up the hill and then in my direction, but they can't see me behind the bush. Then the owner goes back into the café, and Fred stats walking in my direction. As he is walking past me, I come out from behind the bush. He looks amazed at me. 'What do you think you've been doing, throwing stones, you could have killed someone', he said. 'But we were only aiming at the roof', I said. 'You'll have to tell the policeman that when he comes' said Fred. 'I'm going back home to tell Muttie'.

With that he goes back down the hill. I am still thinking of following Wolfgang up the hill, but then decide against it. When I get as far as the Café, I can see the policeman coming up the track, then the café owner comes out and tells me to stop and they start talking together.

Then the policeman waves for me to come to them. 'So where's the other rascal', asks the owner. 'I don't know. He went back in to town the other way'.

'Now you are coming to the police station with me, young man', says the policeman. I am horrified. I think they might lock me up.

We walk down to the police station, which is at the back of the town hall. Luckily there is no one around, because it's lunchtime, otherwise other people might have got to know I've been arrested. At the station the policeman asks my name and address, and whether my parents had a telephone. When I told him we had one, he gets more friendly, but I don't know our number by heart. Then he asks me about Wolfgang, and I tell him where he lives, even though I don't have the house number. Then the policeman says I can go home now, but he will come to the house in the afternoon to have a word with my parents.

When I get home I tell Muttie what has happened. She looks very serious, but when she sees how worried I am, she tells me to go to my room and rest. I really am frightened everybody will be told I have been arrested, including the school. I am worried they might expel me, and I think my whole future might be bad after what happened.

At last I go to sleep, and then I wake up when the front door bell rings. It's the policeman. He spends about a quarter hour with Muttie, and I expect her to call me, but she doesn't. After the policeman is gone, she comes in and tells me that the police have to inform the school, but other than that nothing will happen, provided I never do such a thing again.

I am now feeling much better, and think what we had done wasn't really bad, just stupid. I also wonder what Wolfgang has told his mother, and whether the police had been there too. Later I hear that they had. I think the Winklers are more nervous than Muttie, because Wolfgang is not a good boy like me really.

When I am back at school after the holidays, I am expecting to be called to the headmaster's office. I had been worried about this for a long time, but nothing more happens. I don't even know if my teacher, Herr Gruber, ever found out about it.

This is me in front with my brother Fred behind on the left outside the block of flats in Berlin where we lived

Here we are with Muttie and Papa in our garden in Moedling

Our Doctor Loewe when I last saw him

The nude lady in Moedling Swimming Pool entrance.

Fred and me playing by a brook in the Vienna Woods

Trudl and me looking at the ducklings I got for an Easter present.

Herr Hobiger with sawstika badge

Papa in his Knickerbockers and English cap, and me in my leather shorts on our holiday in the mountains

Muttie and Herr Pawlitschek dancing on the ice on Laxenburg Lake while I am winding the grammophone

Hitler addressing the crowd in Vienna in March 1938. Herbert was there with his brother and parents.

At the Grammar School.

I've started Grammar school. I had to pass an exam and got through easily. Fred has been going there before me, but last year he failed the end of year exams for the second time. He has a problem with Maths and Latin, and doesn't really like studying, so Papa has arranged for him to go to the Moedling Business College instead.

I quite like learning things and showing the teachers that I'm paying attention. Our class teacher is Herr Meyer, who teaches Latin. He is young and very serious. I think he is a Catholic My favourite teacher is Herr Breitschedl. He is also young and always dressed in a smart suit and wears gold rimmed spectacles. He often smiles and makes jokes with us. He takes us for history. We are doing the Roman Empire, and he has been telling us about Hannibal and how he marched his army from Africa through Spain across the Alps into Italy, with Elephants to carry the heavy equipment, and how he nearly defeated the Roman Army in Italy. I think Herr Breitschedl is a Nazi, because he's telling us that Hannibal achieved a lot because like Hitler he wanted to do his best for his people.

Our mathematics teacher is a lot older. He stoops and has a beard and is a bit Jewish looking. We have heard that he was wounded in the war and has a metal plate in the top of his head, although you can't see it through his hair. He has difficulty keeping some of the naughtier boys under control, and they sometimes throw paper darts at him when he is drawing diagrams on the blackboard. Then he turns round and says 'Stand up who did that,.' None of the boys ever stand up, so he says if he ever catches one he will report him to the headmaster. But the boys who did it just snigger, because they know they won't be caught. I feel sorry for him, because he doesn't look a very happy or healthy man, and Jesus teaches us to be kind to others.

We also have an English teacher who has the nickname 'Pinzgauer' because his teeth look a bit like a horse's. He wears thick glasses and is also young and sometimes makes a joke about me being English and having to learn it, but only in a very friendly way. He has actually been to England. In the book we use there is a story about the way the English say things which can be misunderstood by foreigners. It's about a foreign visitor looking out of a train window, and one of the other passengers sees a train coming in the opposite direction. He shouts, 'Look out', whereupon the visitor strains his head further out to see what is coming, and nearly has it knocked off. So we all have a good laugh at that.

In geography we have another young teacher with a moustache and a small beard. He teaches us about the various regions of Austria and how to read and understand maps of the world. Our Art teacher is bald headed with a moustache who likes to paint pictures of horses. He teaches us drawing and painting in a way I don't like. Everything we paint, whether a flower, an animal or a house, has to have a thick black outline. I can't understand why he teaches us like that because I have seen one of his paintings and it looks like real life without any black lines. He is known to be a Nazi, and he is the only teacher who gives me bad marks at the end of the year, just because I don't follow his instruction to put black lines around everything I paint.

In grammar school we now have proper separate religion classes for the Catholics, the Protestants and the Jews. Pastor Mueller takes the Protestant class. There are only twelve of us in the class. He doesn't come to the school every day, but sometimes I meet him on the way there in the morning and he says to me in English, 'Good morning, Master Bush' in reply to my 'Gruess Gott, Herr Pastor'.

Our gym teacher is Professor Hornung. He is a bit older than the other teachers, and he always wears knickerbockers. He walks slowly and never gets angry about anything. Sometimes he helps the more cowardly boys jumping over the wooden horse in the gym. When we play games in courtyard he will only let us play handball, not football, because the ground is hard and gravelled. He likes to blow his whistle when someone is breaking the rules or committing a foul.

We only see the school headmaster when there are meetings in the main assembly hall with all the pupils, like some national celebrations or annual prize givings. But he also has to speak to pupils reported to him for being rude to the teachers, and he can expel a pupil if he thinks it necessary, but he hasn't had to do that since I have been at the school.

Once a year just before the summer holidays, classes go for a walk with their class teacher on a Saturday morning. When we went with Professor Meyer, he brought his fiancée with him. She is a bit younger and heavier than Professor Meyer, but she has a nice smiley face and we can see he is very proud of her. We went into the Vienna Woods towards Baden, and Professor Meyer pointed out the names of plants and birds on the way. Then we sat in a meadow to eat our Salami rolls together. When we got back to Moedling it was getting very hot and we all took off our Jackets, apart from Professor Meyer, even though he was sweating.

Herr Hobiger and the Gym

Herr Hobiger sometimes stops by at our house on his way home from the station in the afternoon when he can leave the office in Vienna early. When I go to open the gate to let him in, he always says something funny to me, like 'Hello lieber latiner' which can mean 'hello latin book' in Latin or 'hello dear latiner' in German, because he knows I always get good marks in Latin in my exams.

He once told Muttie that he used to belong to the 'Turnverein', which was a sort of gymnastics club where they teach you how to do handstands on the parallel bars and somersaults over the horse. He also told her that when he was younger he won a lot of prizes at athletics competitions.. He says in Germany the gymnasts are given proper help by the government because Hitler thinks bodily discipline is important, and they have schemes called 'Strength through Joy' to help people become fit. He is still very fit and thin, even though he no longer does gymnastics.

When I found out that Herr Hornung, our gymnastics teacher at school, has started a gymnastics club at the school which meets every Saturday afternoon in term time, I asked Papa if I could join. It's something to do with a Viennese Club called 'Uranium'. You have to pay to go there, but I like Gym, and what we do as part of our school lessons is pretty boring, because a lot of the other children are really afraid of jumping over the box or climbing up the ropes which I like doing, and I want to become a good gymnast like Herr Hobiger. So Papa has arranged for me to join.

This Saturday I went for the first time. I have to pay Professor Hornung the money Papa has given me, and then I can go into the changing room to put on my black gym shorts and white vest and gym plimsolles.

There are only eight of us, and most of the others are boarders from the orphanage, where they live in term time because their home is too far away from the school. Two of the oldest help to set up the equipment, and stand by when we have to do a hand-jump over the horse, which is what the long box with hand grips in the middle is called. You have to jump on the trampoline first, which is exciting, and then grip the handles and do a somersault, landing on your feet on the mat behind. I'm really proud I can do it, and then I learn to do a handstand and walk on my hands as well.

Herr Hornung stands by and now and again corrects what we are doing, but generally doesn't interfere very much. I think he is too easy going and not very strict, just like a typical Viennese, and he lives in Vienna. I think he always wears plus-fours to show off his bulging muscular legs. I think he is a 'Black', which is what they call supporters of the Catholic led government.

At the end of the session Herr Hornung blows his whistle, and the older boys put away the equipment whilst the rest of us get dressed. I'm only sorry that none of my friends have joined the club. Perhaps their parents can't afford it.

At the cinema

Last week I went to the cinema in Moedling to see an English film called 'Sanders of the River'. Sanders is a British officer in charge of a district in Africa. He wears a pith helmet and big shorts which go down to his knees, and smokes a pipe. He has to sort out a dispute between two local tribes, and the leader of one of the local tribes is called 'Bosambo' and he is played by Paul Robeson, a famous American singer. He gets Sanders to support him in his struggle with the other tribe, and in one of the scenes to celebrate his victory he is being paddled down the river singing a native song which sounds like 'Eye eeh yoh go, eye eeh yo go' repeated over and over in rhythm with the paddle strokes.

Walter also went to see the film, so when he came over to play one afternoon we did this scene from the film in the garden. Walter said I must play the part of Sanders since I was British, and he would play Bosambo, even though he is blond and doesn't look a bit like Paul Robeson. We put some wooden planks on our garden path with cushions for seats, and Walter used a piece of wood as a paddle and pretended to be paddling up the garden path singing 'I eeh yo go'.while I stood by in my leather shorts wearing one of Papa's hats with a stick between my teeth pretending I was smoking a pipe. Walter tried to get his voice as low a Paul Robeson's, but he couldn't keep it low for more than a few verses, and in the end we both laughed so much he couldn't go on with it.

The Earleys have given me a season ticket for the cinema as a Christmas present. I was really thrilled, because I like going to our cinema, and I have seen quite a few English and American films already, but all in German, which can look funny at times when the actors mouths don't move as they should when they are speaking. I also saw a German film called 'Storm flight to Claudia' which was a silly love story about a pilot in Lufthansa to show how clever he was to get his Junker aircraft through a storm and save all the passengers' lives.

I break my arm

Herbert, Walter and me are playing cowboys and Indians in the woods behind the Othmar Church. I am galloping down the slope on my horse, jump off the wall on to the bridle way underneath and slip in the storm water gulley. I try to save myself from falling on to my face with my right arm and twist it. Well, it's more like a kink, really. Herbert says he thinks it's broken, but I don't like to believe that. But there is something sticking out a little which I don't like to touch.

I walk home supporting the right arm with my left one so it doesn't hurt so much. When Muttie sees it she says we must go to the hospital right away, even though I tell her I think it's only twisted. When we get there we have to wait a little while before seeing the doctor, who is Dr Foen, a big smiley man. He takes a quick look at the arm, and says 'You might as well sleep here tonight, young man, and we'll put this right for you tomorrow morning.'

'But I think it's only twisted,' I say.

'Don't worry, we'll untwist it for you tomorrow', he says and smiles at Muttie.

Muttie is allowed to stay with me when the nurse puts me to bed. I'm in the room with two other older children. The Nurse gives me something to swallow and I go off to sleep. Early next morning two men come and put me on a trolley. They say I don't need to worry, soon my arm will be alright. They wheel me into a large room with a lot of lamps and instruments, with Dr. Foen standing there smiling at me. He says 'just lie back and count to ten while we put this over your face to help you go to sleep so we can straighten your arm without you feeling anything'. I can hear something coming out of the mask they put over my mouth and nose, and that's all I remember until I wake up. I am looking straight at Muttie, she is holding my good arm, the other one is in plaster supported by a bandage round my neck.

I have to stay another night at the hospital. Next morning Dr. Foen comes and has a look at me. 'Well, young man, we've straightened out the kink and in a month's time you'll be able to use your arm again just like before. But in the meantime you'll have to keep it in the plaster'

In the afternoon Muttie came to fetch me, and I was able to walk home with her, proudly holding my plastered arm like a soldier coming home from the war.

A couple of weeks later the plaster was cut off at the hospital, and I could see there was a scar. Muttie said Dr Foen had told her it was a compound fracture, and the scar was caused by part of the bone coming out from inside the skin. I was very proud of the scar, and showed it to all my friends. They were very impressed.

Herr Hobiger breaks his neck

A few months after that we are going for our Sunday swim with the Hobigers. This morning we're all in the pool, and Herr Hobiger is there with Frau Hobiger. He wears long black swimming trunks, and just over the top of them I can see the scar on each side of his body where the bullet went through him in the war. But he is very fit and thin compared with Frau Hobiger, who is quite thick around the middle.

Herr Hobiger always dives in head first and puts his arms down by his sides before he hits the water. He does it again this time, but when he comes up for air he looks dazed, and then slowly walks to the steps and gets out of the pool. When I go upstairs to dress later, he is already dressed. He doesnn't say anything and is looking very pale. Then he goes to speak to Herr Eichert, the Swimming Pool attendant. He doesn't turn his head and it looks as though he has got a stiff neck. Herr Eichert looks at his neck and runs his finger along it. He looks very serious and says a few words to Herr Hobiger, then Herr Hobiger picks up his carrier bag with his towel and swim suit and goes out of the swimming pool building, never turning his head.

Herr Eichert later tells Papa to tell Frau Hobiger that he advised Herr Hobiger to go to the hospital right away. He says he hit his head on the bottom of the pool, and he thinks he may have injured his neck. We are all amazed that he is walking to the hospital, because it is over a mile's walk. As soon as Frau Hobiger comes out of the changing rooms, Papa tells her what has happened. She looks very worried and says she is going to follow him to the hospital right away.

Later that afternoon she comes to our house on the way back from the hospital., and tells us that Herr Hobiger has been X-rayed, and that he has fractured a vertebrae in his neck. He will have to have a plaster put around his neck and head to keep it quite still, and he will have to stay in hospital for about a week.. But only four days later I am sitting in the garden in the afternoon reading when the front gate bell rings. I go to have a look and it's Herr Hobiger. He looks like a knight in a white helmet, with everything from his shoulders to the top of his head covered in plaster, with just his face and his ears showing.

But he is quite cheerful and greats me as he always does with 'hello lieber latiner' Muttie is a bit shocked when she sees him, but she pretends not to be and asks him in for coffee. She really likes him and was quite worried about him. After he is gone she tells me that he has to go home and rest for another three weeks before they remove the plaster, and he is worried about his job at the bank. I can't imagine they would give his job to someone else, particularly when he has been so brave. But he told Muttie that you can never be sure with the Jews.

Three weeks later he has the plaster removed, and he goes back to the bank to work, so he hasn't lost his job after all. Perhaps they don't know he is a Nazi. I'm really glad, and after this he sometimes drops in for a chat with Muttie on his way home from the station, because he finishes work in the afternoon, not like Papa who doesn't come home until the evening.

1936

At Church

Pastor Mueller often asks us when we were last at church. I think he knows I often miss out a Sunday morning sevice at the Protestant church, and I feel guilty about it, even though Papa and Muttie don't mind. They never go to Church, except Christmas time to see the nativity play if Fred or I are in it.

Pastor Mueller is a very good speaker. You can understand what he is saying, and it's all about how we should behave towards others. He does bring the Bible into it as well, but in a way that really means something in our everyday life. Last Sunday he was telling us about the poor African children who live in poverty and often have to starve, and he asked us to put something into the collection box for them. He said if we loved Jesus, we should also love all those who have to suffer for no fault of their own.

Sometimes we have an older man with a beard and dressed in a Tyrolean outfit with breeches to talk to the children only, after

Pastor Mueller's sermon. He would get the children together on a separate pew and tell them some stories from the Bible. Then he would explain how they can be applied to our everyday lives. I think he is a nice man, but I sometimes think he is expecting us to be too much like Jesus. Pastor Mueller is more forceful, and I always remember how during one religion lesson he threw the bible at me for not having been at Church the Sunday before because I went swimming instead. I've heard somebody say he is a Nazi, and Herbert has told me that sometimes on a Saturday he can hear him play the organ very loudly, because he lives next to the church. He thinks it's something to do with Pastor Mueller giving his wife a baby. I don't ask Herbert how he does that, because I am ashamed I don't know. He has three children already.

A cycling expedition.

Frau Hobiger has a bicycle, because they live some distance away from the shops. She is visiting Muttie, so I asked her whether I could have a go on her bike while she was talking to Muttie. She let me, after she had asked Muttie. Muttie said yes, because she knew I had ridden a children's bike before, and as long as I didn't go out on to the Schillerstrasse, which is the main road at the end of our road, it would be OK. I managed to get on to the pedals because it was a ladies' bike, but I couldn't sit on the saddle, so I had to cycle by just standing on the pedals. I managed it alright, but I couldn't turn it around without getting off the bike first.

When Papa found out that I had learnt to ride a bike, he arranged for me and Fred to go on a cycle trip with him on bikes hired from a shop in Moedling. We cycled all the way to Laxenburg where we had been skating in the winter. It's got lots of woods and a lake, and we could get there in about half an hour. On the way we passed the factories where they make bricks with the clay from the brick ponds, and also a lot of workers' houses for poor people who worked there. We knew that they were all Sozis, and were probably supporting the workers who tried to take over the government. There were some children playing out on the road, and when we cycled past they stopped playng and just stood looking at us. They knew that we were rich, because only rich people can afford bicycles, and I could see that they didn't like us for that reason alone. I was glad when we got away from the houses into the open flat country with large fields before we got to the Laxenburg Palace at the entrance to the Park. We had to leave our bikes at the entrance, but we took a walk into the Park. It's got a lot of very big trees, and rivers and canals and a lake with a castle on an island called the Franzenburg. Papa took some photographs with his new Rolleiflex camera, which he is very proud of. He does a lot of photography, and he does all his own developing and printing. Quite often when we go for walks in the mountains, he makes us all stand still to take pictures of us, and sometimes he puts the camera on a tripod and a timer so he can stand with us and be in the picture. But this time he only took pictures of some of the statues in the park.

On the way back we cycled quickly through the place with the workers' houses because we didn't like being stared at by all those children. But they didn't dare to shout any rude words, because Papa was wearing his plus-fours, so they knew he was important.

At the Gerichtsberg.

Near the end of our summer holidays I am going to stay with Herbert Krisch and his brother Ernsti at the Gerichtsberg where Herbert's mother's family own a small farm. It's in the Vienna Woods about an hour's ride from Moedling. Herbert's uncle has come to pick me up on his motorbike, and I am going to ride on the pillion saddle behind him. It's a really big and modern motorbike, and it makes a big noise when he speeds it up. I'm a little frightened about sitting on the pillion seat behind Herbert's uncle, because I have never really met him before. But he is very friendly, a big man with grey hair and wearing a long motorcycling mac and goggles. I am carrying all my things in my rucksack, but there is not a lot in it because I am only staying there for a week, and then Herbert's uncle will come and fetch me back.

Muttie looks a bit worried about my having to sit on the saddle for all that time, but I tell her I am quite comfortable, and

Herbert's uncle tells me to put my arms around his waist and to squeeze it if I want him to stop for anything. Then we start up the road with a roar and I wave goodbye to Muttie.

It seems quite a long drive, but it's a really sunny day and there is a lot to see on the way. We ride through villages and along river valleys on the way, and we can see all the cows and sheep grazing on the hillsides. Some of the time we are going along a railway line, and we can see steam trains puffing clouds of smoke into the sky.

When we are nearly there we turn up a side road which goes uphill, and then over a level crossing over a railway line. Then Herbert's uncle points ahead and I can see a farmhouse a little way up the hill, with a big balcony running right along the front and the sides. It's on a slope so the ends of the balcony are at gound level. We can see people on the balcony waving, and as we pull into the farmyard Herbert and Ernsti come running over shouting hello.

Then we all go through the entrance hall into the sitting room, and there are Herr and Frau Krisch and Herberts mother's sister, who also lives in Moedling, and her daughter, Herbert's cousin Margaret. She is just about the same age as us, and she is a little bigger around the middle but not really fat. She has very dark hair and eyebrows, and dark brown eyes like her mother's, and she looks serious but smiles when she talks to you.

After Herbert and Ernsti have shown me our bedroom, they take me into the farmyard and show me the stables and the meadows where the cows are grazing. They tell me that the farmer and his wife and their daughter Heidi, who is also the same age as us, live on the ground floor underneath the floor we are on.

The next day Herbert's uncle leaves early to ride back to Moedling. Frau Krisch gives us bread rolls with dripping, my favourite breackfast. Then we do some more exploring round the farm. Herbert takes us up the hill to the boundary fence of their property, right through the cows grazing in the fields. I'm a bit scared of them, but Herbert says they are nothing to be frightened of.

The rest of the morning we have a look at the stables, and then we play hide and seek around the farm. We have goulash for lunch, and Margaret helps her mum and aunt with the cooking and serving. After lunch she goes downstairs to talk to Heidi, the farmer's daughter. Herr Krisch has brought some papers with him and has to work in the room at the back of the farmhouse. Later in the afternoon us boys go down to the level crossing when we hear a train coming up the valley. The crossing gates have come down, and we hang on to them waiting for the train. It gives a loud whistle to let everyone know it's coming, and when the engine goes past the driver waves to us and we wave back. It's a single track line so it's only slow trains and goods trains that go past, and the drivers get to know the people along the line.

In the evening us boys and Margaret have our supper separately from the grownups, so we can talk and make a lot of noise without disturbing them. Then we can go out and play until it gets dark. We are allowed to stay up and play ping-pong on a table in the living room till nine o'clock, then we can go to our bedroom and read in bed. Herbert has hidden a torch on the shelf over his bed, and after Frau Krisch has come in and switched off the light, he puts on the torch under his duvet to read his book. Then he puts his head over the duvet and shines the torch on to his face from under his chin and he looks just like a monster. We all have a go at this, until Frau Krisch hears our giggling and comes in to take Herbert's torch and tells us to go to sleep. But she isn't really cross, she is always smiley and friendly.

Next day Frau Krisch tells me to go to her at ten o'clock, because she has arranged with Mutti for me to speak to her on the telephone then to let her know I'm alright. I'm not used to the telephone, so she rings Muttie first and tells her everything is fine, then she shows me how to hold the phone and speak into it. Mutti says hello and asks if I am enjoying myself, and what we have been doing. I can't think of much to tell her, so she just asks me questions and I just answer yes or no. After that Mutti asks me to give the phone back to Frau Krisch, who talks some more with her and tells her she will ring again next Sunday morning after she has had a talk with her brother about what time he will be taking me back home.

The rest of the week just goes by very quickly. I get to know Heidi, who is about the same age as Margaret, one year older than me. She wears a plain coloured dirndl and has light brown hair and blue eyes and I think she is quite pretty, but I don't understand some of the things she says because she speaks with a local dialect. She and Margaret come out to play hide and seek with us boys, and also 'catch' when whoever is 'it' has to find the ones hiding and try to touch them before they can get to 'home', which is a tree on its own near the farmhouse.

Heidi laughs more than Maragaret, and she screams when we are chasing her when we are 'it'. Later we boys also try to do rope skipping, which the girls do a lot of the time, but we can't do it as well as they can. We are better at rolling down the hill where the grass has been cut. I think the girls are a bit shy about showing their knickers when they are doing this. After supper most evening we boys play a board game called 'just don't get annoyed, man'. Sometimes Margaret plays with us, and sometimes even the grownups play it with us.

On Sunday afternoon Herbert's uncle takes me back home to Spechtgasse in Moedling. I'm sad to have to say goodbye to Heidi and Margaret and everybody, but I'm looking forward to seeing Papa and Muttie again. When I get back home, Muttie gives me a big hug, but not Papa, because men don't do that kind of thing. I think they are quite proud that I can stay with friends without them for a whole week, which even Fred has never done. I am quite proud of myself as well.

Evenings out

Muttie is keen to stay in touch with German people here, because both her parents are German. When she was a girl, she belonged to 'the Migrator Birds', an organisation for students who go around playing mandolins and singing folk songs in public to help them pay for their wandering through Germany on their holidays. I think she feels more German than Papa, even though the Austrians speak the same language, but with a different dialect. She doesn't like me speaking the Viennese dialect, particularly when we boys are shouting it in the garden, because she has been brought up to speak 'High German' and thinks the dialect is coarse and shows that you haven't been educated properly. My Austrian friends think it's a bit like making out we are a better class of people, but they make allowance for my parents because they are really foreign.

Once we went to a beer evening organised by the 'Bund', the Association of Reich Germans, at the hotel near the station with the Winklers and the Kochs, who are German. There were a lot of people there, and we all sat in rows of tables. Everybody apart from the children drank beer, and the waitresses were kept busy all evening just bringing it to the tables. Then some important German men got up and made speeches about how important it was for Austria to keep its cultural ties with Germany.

Then there was some singing of German folk songs, and the evening ended with everybody standing up to sing the German national anthem, 'Germany, Germany over all'. I don't think Papa enjoyed it that much, he prefers the evenings at the 'Heurigen' (which means 'this year's wine) – where they play what they call 'Schrammel' music with an accordion. On the way home he said to Muttie he thought a lot of the people at the beer evening were Nazis. Although he doesn't have anything against them, he thinks we shouldn't take sides, particularly since he was really British and we are all registered as British citizens at the Consulate, even though only he can speak English. I don't think Muttie agrees, but she never argues with Papa.

Papa doesn't talk much about politics, except once I overheard him telling a friend that he belongs to the 'Pan Europa' movement to form Europe into a sort of 'United Sates'. I think that's what the Nazis are really doing anyway, except that they want all the countries to be united under Germany.

This evening we are going to a Heurigen at Gumpoldskirchen, which is famous for its local wine. We are going together with the Earleys and the Winklers, including Wolfgang, and we had to get there by train, even though it's only one stop. Fred and I like it just because we can go on the railway. At the Heurigen the children drink apple juice or lemonade, but all the grown-ups drink wine. Soon everyone is quite merry, and some of the people there get up and dance to the accordion, but not from our group, since Herr Winkler can't dance because of his artificial leg. Wolfgang and Fred and I can go and play in the courtyard, where they have a couple of friendly German Shepherd dogs.

Afterwards we have to walk back to the station by lamplight, and everybody is laughing at Herr Winkler's jokes, even the women, apart from Frau Winkler, who doesn't enjoy her husband's jokes. On the train there are a lot of people who have also been to the Heurigen, and some of the men are a bit noisy and unsteady on their legs, but nobody in our group.

Arabian nights with Trudl

Sometimes when the Hobigers come to visit us on Sunday afternoons, Trudl comes into our playroom which is also our bedroom and has the ping-pong table in it. Fred and me sometimes play ping-pong with Trudl, but today Fred is visiting one of his friends. Trudl and I are talking about Sonia Henji, the Austrian ice dancing star. Then I have an idea – we can get on the ping- pong table and pretend it is an ice rink and skate on it. Trudl says but what about the music? So I go into the living room where the grownups are and ask Papa if we can have the wind- up gramophone and a waltz record. He brings it into the playroom and shows us how to use it. He doesn't know we are going to play ice dancing on the ping pong table, because I don't tell him in case he won't let us.

When the music starts, we get on to the table without our shoes on and pretend to be skating. Trudl makes a pirouette and nearly falls off the table, but in a little while we can both pretend to do a proper waltz on the table, but not together. When the music finishes, we both clap. Then we have another go and it's really quite good, even though we have to be careful not to fall off. But my bed and Fred's settee are quite close to the table, so if we fall off the sides we would fall on to the beds.

After a while we get tired and lie down on Fred's settee together. Trudl is reading one of my 'Butterfly' children's magazines, and I am reading a chapter from 'The Arabian nights' where it said something about an Arabian prince sleeping with a princess. I am beginning to think it's got something to do with making babies, but I can't understand why they have to sleep when they are doing this. I look at Trudl but don't say anything about this. I'm just embarrassed about asking her about things like that. While I am wondering what would happen if we both drop off to sleep, I notice that my willie is beginning to swell up a bit, and it's quite a nice feeling. Perhaps this has got something to do with making babys, because I am lying right next to Trudl and our bodies are touching. I have a look down at my leather shorts, but I don't think anybody can see what's happened to my willie, and of course I don't say anything to Trudl, who is still reading the magazine.

1937

A New Year's Eve Party

Tonight we are having a New Year's party. The Earleys are coming with their daughter Edie, who is visiting them, and Mr and Mrs Finlayson, the Winklers, and Fraeulein Tomanek with a new man friend from her University. Papa has planned it all to start with a bang at eight o'clock in the evening. Everybody is taken through the dining room with the lights switched off, into the lit-up cabinet room. Then Papa has to wait for some of them who are late. In the meantime there is silence in the cabinet room, because some of the people in it don't know each other. This makes Mr Earley chuckle, but then Herr Winkler introduces himself and Frau Winkler and Wolfgagng to Fraeulein Tomanek and her friend, who I think must be her boyfriend, and to the Earleys and Edie, who is short but quite good looking, and I think Fred really likes her, even though she is older than him.

Now the Finlaysons have come, and as soon as they are in the cabinet room, Papa plays a few loud chords on the piano, Mutti switches on all the lights in the dining room and Papa opens a bottle of champagne with a loud pop. The floor has been cleared for dancing, with the Christmas tree and the dining table in the corner. Papa puts on a record of Christmas music, and Fred and I have to take a tray with champagne glasses around to everybody. Papa proposes a toast to 'The New Year', and soon everybody is chatting away. Then Papa puts on some records of waltzes on our gramophone and Fraeulein Thomanek and her new friend start dancing and then the others join in, except the Earleys and Herr Winkler who can't dance because of his leg. They sit in the cabinet room and talk together.

Now it's ten o'clock. Fred and I take Wolfgang into our playroom to play with our electric train set, which is laid out on the Ping- Pong table. There are some toy soldiers on it as well, with two tanks that can fire match sticks. The soldiers are Italians and Abyssinians, and they are fighting each other from trenches on opposite sides of the table. First we put our soldiers on the train which takes them around to their trenches, which are like the ones they had in the first World War. Fred and Wolfgang are on the Italian side, and I am on the Abyssinian side on the opposite side of the table. We stand our soldiers up, some inside the trenches and some running firing flamethrowers at the other side. We light the matches and fire them at the other side, but they go out before they hit their targets. They can't even knock the soldiers over, so we wind up the tanks and let them move across the table at the opposite trenches. Then some of the soldiers are knocked over, and we count who has knocked more soldiers over to see who won.

Later on Muttie calls us to go down with the grownups into the basement where she has laid out tables and chairs, and we have a supper of frankfurters or rollmops and potato salad with gherkins, my favourite meal next to roast goose, and then pineapple slices. Fraeulein Tomanek and her boyfriend are sitting together and are talking to each other. I think they are in love.

Later everybody goes back upstairs. Then at twelve o'clock Papa plays a Scottish tune called 'Aud Lang Syne' on the piano. The Earleys and the Finlaysons who know the English words sing along, then we all shake hands and wish each other Happy New Year, and then all the grownups drink more wine. Then the

Winklers leave with Wolfgang, and Fred and I have to say good night to everybody and go to bed. But we can still hear the party going on until we fall asleep.

Not long after the party at Carnival time Muttie and Papa are going to the Mask Ball at the Hofburg palace in Vienna. It's really for rich people, but Papa thinks they should go just this once. They have to dress in their best evening dress, and Muttie has to have a mask to put on because until midnight all the ladies have to wear a mask, and they choose who they dance with. Then after midnight they can dance with their partners again.

Next day we hear Muttie telling Fraeulein Anna that they had a very nice time,and she is already looking forward to going to the Mask Ball again next year. When they tell the Hobigers about their adventure, they are very impressed. They must think Papa is quite rich to be able go to the Hofburg. I don't think we are rich, really, but Papa doesn't save money like a lot of other people. Herr Hobiger jokes about Muttie wearing her mask at the Ball, and asks her whether she enjoyed dancing with a lot of strange men. Muttie goes red in the face and says she didn't dance with any strange men. When Herr Hobiger asks Papa if he danced with other ladies, he just smiles and says that will have to remain a state secret.

I punch a Sozi

Since I started going to Grammar school I often see some of the children coming back from the Secondary school. There are a couple of them who always make faces and cock a snoot at me. I think it's because they are jealous that I go to the grammar school, or maybe it's because I don't wear leather shorts to school. I try not to get close to them, but one time I did, and one of them, a ginger- haired boy, swung his satchel at me and nearly knocked me over. Then they both ran off, laughing and jeering. Now I'm careful to keep my distance from them. I think they are probably Sozis, because they walk further on down across the level crossing to the housing estate where all the people are working class.

Recently I've been reading a book about a German adventurer who travels in the tropics. He has a big negro servant who is very strong and helps to protect his master, and often the stories are about how he rescues his master when he gets into a dangerous situation. In the last story I am reading, the adventurer is on a motor yacht, and he has been shot from another yacht by some smugglers he tried to stop. The negro had swum across to the other yacht, but was found and taken prisoner, so the hero is on his own. He is lying on his bunk in the yacht bandaging the gun wound in his arm, when he realises that the other yacht is coming alongside. So he reaches for the pistol in the holster he carries under his arm and creeps up on deck. Just then one of the smugglers is about to jump on to his yacht, so he shoots him and he falls into the sea. In the meantime the negro has managed to free himself and throws the other smuggler into the sea.

I think how brave the adventurer was to crawl back on deck with his wounded arm, and I intend to become braver as well. I start testing myself by driving on my scooter into a heap of gravel we have in the garden, going as fast as I can. Then I think I should test my courage with the Sozi boys.

Next time I see them coming along after school, I slow down and wait for them to catch me up. The ginger one is grinning at me, but I think he realises something is happening from the way I have stopped and am looking at him. Then I run towards him, raise my fist over his head and bring it down with a thump. He is so surprised that he just stands there looking at me, so I turn around and run off as fast as I can. I don't think I have really hurt him much, but I didn't feel brave enough to stop and find out. After that they don't try to hit me with their satchels, but they still jeer at me.

Yesterday I met Pastor Mueller on our way to school. This time he slowed down to talk to me. 'So', he said to me, 'and what does your father think of the Duke of Windsor?' I was embarrassed because I had to tell him I didn't know. Papa doesn't discuss things like that with Fred or me. But I realised why Pastor Mueller wanted to know. Herbert had told me he thinks he is a Nazi, so he was interested to know what an Englishman thinks about the Duke meeting Hitler and being friendly with him.

I think the Duke of Windsor is a very modern Englishman, and he has the right idea to be friendly with Hitler. Perhaps he wants to make England National Socialist as well. There have been a lot of pictures and articles about him in the papers, and some show him talking to quite ordinary people, like dockers and miners. I think the rest of his family don't like that – they want to have all the power to themselves, and not share it with their countrymen like Hitler. I think Mrs Simpson, or the Duchess, is also a very modern woman, not like the Duke's family who live in the past.

Papa loses his job.

Papa has stopped going to the office. The Western Electric company, the American company he was working for, has closed its office in Vienna. It's something to do with a court case against the company by a German company which also makes sound film equipment, but hasn't been allowed to sell in Austria and some other countries in Europe because Western Electric had the only rights to sell this equipment in these countries. The German company has won its case, and started selling their equipment much cheaper than Western Electric could sell it for, so Western Electric's offfice in Vienna was closed down.

Now Papa still sometimes goes to Vienna, but it's something to do with an invention he has made. It's for a game called 'Lexicon', where each player is given a number of square plastic discs with letters on them and grooves in their sides so they can link up with each other, and then take turns to make words with them. Papa has to have a demonstration model made, which is quite expensive, and he has to tell the manufacturers how he wants it made. He is also going to England to see if he can find someone there to manufacture and sell the game. In the meantime he spends a lot of his time on a typewriter, because he is also writing a book about his life, and how he came to be in the German army during the war. He is going to call it 'A son of two nations'.

It's quite exciting because he was really English and born and brought up in London, even though his father was German. But his father wanted Papa to learn German and sent him to be apprenticed at the American Chamber of Commerce in Berlin. Papa was working there when the war started, and according to German Law he was German, so he was called up into the army. He had already met Muttie, so he must have thought he should be on the German side for her sake.

Now Papa is going to London and he will stay there with his mother, who is English and has a boarding house in London. Papa's father had died at the beginning of the last war, so my grandmother set up this boarding house to support herself and Papa's two sisters.

When Papa came back from his visit, he brought me a cardboard model of the new Queen Mary, the biggest ship in the world. Each layer of cardboard was for a separate deck, and had a plan of everything that was on that deck. I spent a long time taking it all apart and looking at how the ship was built. Then I made a wooden model of it, using a piece of wood I found in the toolbox made for Papa by the carpenter next door. I painted it to make it look like the picture of the Queen Mary I had, but it didn't float upright so I didn't show it to anybody.

Papa hasn't found anyone to take up his invention in England, and has tried to find someone in Austria, but no one is interested, so he has decided that this Christmas will be the last one we have in Austria.

1938

At the Krisch Family.

In January Papa and Fred went over to London to live with our Grandmother while they are looking for a job. Muttie is selling some of our furniture, and will be going on to Berlin to stay with her brother Paul until the end of my school term in July. In the meantime I am going to live with the Krisch family. Then Muttie will come and fetch me so we can go on to London together.

Mrs Findlayson has agreed to take Peter, my guinea pig, and look after it. She is now living alone in the flat near the station. I think she is separated from her husband. She has told Muttie I can visit her and Peter any time.

Muttie helps me to pack all my clothes and school things, and then we go to the Krisch's flat in the house on the hill not far from the Protestant Church. The house has a large garden where Herbert and Ernsti, his brother, and I can play. On the opposite side of the road there are only the fences at the ends of the gardens of houses along the road further down, so it's really a nice quiet area. Muttie has a talk with Frau Krisch while Herbert and Ernsti help to carry my things into the room I am going to share with them. They have put in an extra bed for me, but even so there's plenty of space for all of us, and the window looks out over the garden. It's quite a big flat, with two big bedrooms, a large kitchen, a dining room and lounge, and a large veranda where we have our meals.

Later I help Muttie to carry her cases to Moedling station. From there she is going to the main station in Vienna, and then to the Western Station by taxi to catch the train to Berlin. I feel like crying because I won't see her again for four months. I don't think Muttie is very happy either, but she tries to sound cheerful when she kisses me goodbye. 'You wait', she says, 'the time will go by like a flash and I'll be standing here giving you a hello kiss'. And then she is gone.

Frau Krisch welcomes me when I get back. I know she realises how I feel, and she tries to cheer me up. She is nice looking and smiley and always busy. She belongs to a local choir, and often goes out to practice in the evenings, or meets other members just for a chat. She also has quite a few relatives in the town, her sister with husband and daughter Margaret who live in a flat right next to the town square, and her brother who lives in the next town. She is always lively and chatty, and quite different from Herr Krisch, who never says very much. He wears clip-on spectacles and is always well dressed. I have never seen him in leather shorts. He doesn't laugh much, but he always has a little smile when he talks to me. When he is at home he likes to read the papers or listen to the radio.

First thing In the morning before we go off to school Frau Krisch gives us a cup of cocoa and a buttered roll. When we get home from school at lunchtime we have a hot meal with soup and then maybe a schnitzel or a Gulash. In the evening we have a salad, and bread with cream cheese or dripping. Frau Krisch is a good cook and she does everything quickly and without any fuss.

On schooldays we do our homework after school in the afternoon, then we can go out to play in the garden or up in the woods. After supper Frau Krisch goes to see friends, or has friends to visit, mostly women from the choir or relatives. On Sundays we sometimes get visits from Herr Krisch's elder brother from Vienna. I think his wife died some years ago. He always brings chocolades for Herbert and Ernsti, and now also for me. He is a friendly man and usually stays until the late afternoon.

Sometimes I hear Herr Krisch talking to Frau Krisch and criticising the Mayor of Moedling, who we all know is a strong Catholic and a 'black', over the way he is handling things to do with making work for the unemployed or the way he arranges contracts for his political friends for doing unnecessary things around the town.

Herbert has a great interest in javelin throwing. It started at the time of the Olympic games in Germany two years ago. Yesterday was his birthday, and his father has asked him to go choose a javelin at the shop. So Herbert and Ernst and Herr Krisch and me go off to the local sports shop which is owned by a Jew. Herbert looks at the javelins and he picks one which is not too expensive, though they are all very expensive. Herr Krisch just says you have to expect that if you buy from Jews, but there are no other sports shops in Moedling.

Later in the week we go to the field near the Richardhof where we can throw the javelin and there are no other people around in the evening. We pretend we are at the Olympic games, and have a proper competition. Herbert can throw further than me or Ernsti, and is declared the winner. He stands on a rock which is meant to be like a podium, and we start singing the Austrian National Anthem, but then Herbert gives the Nazi salute and shouts 'Heil Hitler' and we all fall about laughing

This evening when we get home, both Herr Krisch and Frau Krisch are listening to the radio. Schuschnigg, the Austrian Chancellor, is speaking. He is telling us that there will be a referendum to decide whether or not Austria will become a part of Hitler's Third Reich.

Herr Krisch just smiles and says they can save themselves the trouble, this will be the end of the Black regime. Now we can expect to see some changes for the better. I've also heard that our doctor Loewe will no longer be allowed to treat non-Jewish patients like me. I think that's really silly, because he has always been a good doctor. I think the Nazis will probably change all that when they realise this.

Anschluss

After that everything happens quickly. We hear that the German Army has started to cross the borders and is occupying Austria. On Thursday when we get home from school there is a crowd in the main square, and schortly after that some German troops in special lorries called personnel carriers roll through on the way to the Moedling Technical College, where they will be stationed. A lot of people are clapping or giving the Nazi salute, and some women are throwing flowers at the soldiers, who just grin and wave. They look very smart in their uniforms, much smarter than the Austrian army looked in their big steel helmets, or the 'Home Defence Corps used to look with their funny caps with feathers stuck in them.

That evening when it gets dark Herbert and Ernsti and I are allowed to go up to the hill over the quarry, where they have started a fire. There are fires on all the hills and mountains in Austria, to celebrate what they call 'the Anschluss'(the Annexation), meaning the joining up of Austria with Germany. There are only two men there feeding the fire from logs which they must have carried up earlier. They are both wearing brown shirts and breeches, and we don't know them. We have never seen Nazis in SA uniform, and we are wondering where they got them from. They are friendly and making jokes in Viennese dialect, and let us help them keeping the flames going, which are about 3 meters high already. When we look out over the adjoining hills we can see fires on every one. Then we get bored just watching the fires and go back into the main square to Frau Krisch's sister's flat, where Herbert's parents are. The flat is up on the first floor, and looks right out over the square. The grownups are standing looking out of the windows into the square, where a German Army band has started playing. They play marches and other music with a lot of drums and bells, quite different from the music the Austrian bands used to play there. Then the grownups sit down and drink wine. Later Herr Krisch stands up and makes a toast to 'the future', and they all look very happy.

Next day at school we have a surprise. When Herr Meyer comes into the class to start the lesson, he said we will now start the day in a different way. Then he raises his right arm and says 'Heil Hitler', and we have to say it all together. He is looking a little strange. I don't think he really likes doing this. Then later on, when we have our art class, our art teacher, Herr Wiedmann who is known to be a Nazi, asks us to draw something about the Anschluss. I draw a picture of a tank, because I have seen some pictures of German tanks in the papers, with the tank commander standing in the turret. Although Herr Wiedmann has always given me bad marks because I don't like drawing everything with a big black outline, which he always tells us to do, he praises my picture and shows it to the class, telling them this is more like what they should be doing.

Later that week I notice that some of our Jewish class mates are being pushed around during break time when there are no teachers around. The ones doing the pushing are the ones who are usually better at sports than at learning things like Latin. I don't really like this, and in any case I have been sharing my desk with Weiss, who is Jewish, for two years now. We have been quite friendly, and I have even been to the flat where he lives once in the afternoon. But I don't say anything to the bully who has been doing most of the pushing, because I'm afraid of him.

There have also been some cases where Jewish shopkeepers in the town have been made to write on their shop windows that they are Jews to warn non Jewish people not to shop there. Herbert says it serves them right for charging so much for the javelin he got for his birthday. But the people who stand around and jeer when the shopkeepers are being made to do these things are mostly uneducated poor people, more like the Sozis.

Today is a holiday, and the Krisch family is going to Vienna to hear Hitler make a speech from the City Hall balcony. Herr Krisch said I should go to visit Mrs Findlayson instead, as she had already invited me. He said that since my parents were not there and I was really English he didn't think it was right that I should have come along anyway. A lot of people are already waiting at the tram station when they leave.

Mrs Findlayson has a little first floor flat in a small white houseat the bottom end of the Schillerstrasse. It has a balcony overlooking the road, and you can see the railway station in the distance. She has made some soup and nice Marmite sandwiches which she knows I really like, because it's something Muttie couldn't get at our local shop where we usually did our shopping. She keeps my Guinea pig Peter in his box in her living room, and Peter looks well and makes his usual squeeking noises when I get him out of the box and stroke him. Mrs Findlayson says it is OK to let him run around the room, even though he sometimes leaves some droppings. She asks me if I have heard from my parents, and I tell her about the postcards I have had from papa in London and Muttie in Berlin. She tells me the Earleys are thinking of selling their shoe business because they think this will be a good time to retire and go back to England, what with all the changes taking place in Vienna.

When I get back to the Krisch's flat there is no one there, so I read one of my Karl May books. When they get back it is already eight o'clock in the evening, and Frau Krisch makes supper. Herr Krisch is looking happy, and he goes to read his Paper. Herbert tells me about the crowd in the Vienna City square, and how after Hitler had made his speech they were all shouting Sieg Heil for a long time. He says his father was so happy he was almost in tears, and he told him and Ernsti that now things really will get better.

The German army command stationed at the Federal Technical college have told the Mayor of Moedling they are having an open day for locals to visit and find out more about what the army is doing. So today I am going with Herbert, Ernsti, Frau Krisch and a woman friend of hers from the choir to the army base. There are already a lot of people at the base, waiting to be taken around by a guide. When our turn comes, a young soldier picks just the five of us and asks us to follow him on to the parade ground, where there are several rows of tanks lined up. He is actually a tank driver, and wears a very smart uniform. He is blond and has blue eyes, and doesn't look much older than eighteen. He speaks in a North German dialect which is a bit difficult for us to understand, and I think he is a bit shy and embarrassed by Frau Krisch and her friend, who are wearing their best dresses and smiling at him.

He doesn't say very much except that he will show us how the tanks work and how they are driven. First he takes us to one of the tanks on the field, and we walk around it while he tells us about how much they weigh, how thick the armour plate is, how much fuel they carry, and what size the gun on the turret is. Then he climbs up and opens the hatch, and then asks Frau Krisch and her friend to climb in first, because there is only room for two people at a time. The ladies climb up and we can see that the young soldier is blushing when they have to lift their legs to get them over the turret hatch, because we can see a long way up their shiny silk stockings. I think the ladies are really enjoying themselves, they are looking at each other and giggling, but try not to embarrass the young soldier too much.

When it comes to our turn, he lets the three of us climb in together. We are surprised at how little we can see from the driver's seat, but he tells us that they quickly get used to the narrow viewing slits, and how they can manoeuvre the tank accurately by applying the brakes alternatively to the left or the right hand tracks. It's very cramped inside, just room for the driver and the gunner and ammunition. Just before we get out, he starts up the engine for us to let us realise how noisy it is inside the tank, and with the hatch open we can already smell the exhaust fumes.

Afterwards Frau Krisch asks him where he is from, and he tells us the name of some small town in Germany none of us have heard of. When we say good bye he just stands to attention and salutes.

The next day when Herr and Frau Krisch have gone out, we play at being tank drivers in the living room. Herbert and Ernsti are pretending to be in the tank barricaded behind a couple of large seat cushions on the couch, and I am attacking using our bedroom slippers as missiles. Quite a few of them hit the wall behind Herbert and Ernsti, and it isn't until later on we realise the slippers left a lot of marks on the wallpaper. Next day Frau Krisch notices the marks and asks Herbert what he knows about them. When Herbert explains to her what happened, and I tell her it was really my fault, her frown turns into a little smile, and she tells us not to do it again, and if we play at tanks to do it in the garden. She is really kind and hardly ever gets angry. Just the other day, I was walking past the open door of Herr and Frau Krische's bedroom thinking I was alone in the flat, but Frau Krisch was just dressing and stood there in her corset and bra looking at me in surprise. Then she just smiled and waved her hand for me to close the door.

Through a friend of hers Frau Krisch has got to know a Russian Woman who has invited us all for coffee on Sunday at her flat. It turns out that she and her husband are refugees, and they are living with their daughter who is about eleven years old in a tiny flat not very far from the Krisch's.

The couple speak German quite well, and it turns out that the husband is working at the University teaching Russian. They managed to escape after he was sent to Vienna to act as interpreter at the Russian Embassy. Herr Krisch is very interested in what they are telling him about what is going on in Russia, how poor the people are, how they are always being watched for anti Bolshevic behaviour and sent off to Siberian Camps as punishment if they are found guilty of even the slightest anti- government criticism. Afterwards Herr Krisch says it all confirms what he has already heard about the Bolshevic way of life. He says it must be like hell on earth, and we should do everything we can to help these poor people. I think we should, too, and I am already a little in love with the Russian girl, who is really pretty.

I think the Nazis are right in not liking the Communists after what we have learnt about them, so the next time I send a postcard to Muttie I ask her if uncle Paul has changed his political beliefs yet, since I had heard Muttie saying he was a Sozi.

Today Papa came back to Moedling to sort out the rest of our belongings with Fraeulein Tomanek. He took me out for lunch, and then we went for a walk around the town. He surprised me by asking whether I wanted to come over to England for good in July, or if I wanted to continue staying with the Krisch family afterwards and carry on studying at the grammar school. I didn't really have to think about it, I knew I wanted to live with him and Muttie. I think he was looking at it the way the Earlys did with their children, who only come to visit them at holiday times. I wouldn't really like that. I think Papa understood, and it was left that I would come to England for good with Muttie in July.

Now it's getting close to the school holidays. We've been told that Field Marshall Goering has been visiting Vienna, and will be leaving today in his blue train, which was designed for him to show off his blue and white uniform. We know he will be travelling on the Southern Railway, because he is visiting other cities along the line. So us boys are going to climb up to the Matterhoerndl, which is a rock sticking out of the hill in the Vienna Woods overlooking Moedling, from which we will be able to see the train. It's about an hour's walk from Moedling, and the rock is quite close to the forestry track. When we get to it, we find it's not as easy to climb as we thought. But we don't really need to, because we can see the railway line down in the valley through the trees. We know the train will be going past around eleven o'clock, so we are prepared for it when it comes. It's really light blue, and we all shout 'Heil Goering' and laugh when we see it.

With Mrs Findlayson

Today Herbert is with the Hitler Youth, but without Ernsti, who is too young, or me because I can't belong because I am British. They learn about camping and marching, and they have to wear black shorts and brown shirts. It's a bit like the Boy Scouts used to be, really, except that they didn't have to do much marching. But in the Hitler Youth you don't have to wear those funny looking hats and long shorts.

I am going to see Mrs Findlayson for tea. I like Mrs Findlayson, even though she is Jewish. I sometimes wonder what she is thinking about what is happening to some of her Jewish friends. Of course since she is British, and has a British passport, she is not directly affected.

It's a really hot afternoon. When I get to her, I find she has a guest, a tall serious looking man about the same age as her. I know it's not her husband. But she doesn't introduce us. She asks me to stay in the flat and play with Peter, and then goes down into the garden with the stranger. Now and again, when I look into the garden, they are walking up and down talking. Both are looking worried.

Just then I can hear a regular drum beat. I go to the window, and I can see a troop of Hitler Youth coming down the road towards the station. They are carrying a flag with a Swastika on it, but it's not streaming in the wind, it's just hanging down. As they march past, I can see Herbert and Walter in their uniforms. They both look very hot and sweaty. They don't know I am here watching them, because I haven't opened the balcony door. I would feel strange if they saw me. Eventually they disappear around the bend, and the drum beat gets fainter and fainter. In a way, I wish I were marching with them. It must be good to belong.

Later Mrs Findlayson comes back upstairs alone. She says she is sorry to have left me on my own, but she had an important matter to talk about with her friend. He is Jewish, and he is asking her to help him to get to England. She shakes her head sadly. 'I've had to tell him there is nothing I can do, because I don't know any important people there', she says.

Then she brings me my favourite Marmite sandwiches and some English tea. She tells me that the Earleys have put their house up for sale, even though they haven't sold their business yet. Their younger son Boysie will be visiting them as usual later in July. It will be after I go to England with Muttie, so I won't see him. Anyway, he was really Fred's friend. I ask her if she is planning to go back to England. She smiles and says not for a while, because she has to look after Peter.

I had really forgotten about what's going to happen with Peter. I know Papa had said he can't come to England because there are a lot of difficult regulations about bringing in animals. Now I'm sad because if Mrs. Findlayson does go back to England, she will have to find someone else to take Peter, and I don't think the Krischs will have him, because they never had pets for Herbert and Ernsti.

Mrs Findlayson asks me what I have been doing, and I tell her about the Russian refugees and what Herr Krisch has been saying about the Communists, and how he thinks the Nazis are really going to change things in Austria. She looks at me sadly and says 'yes, I'm sure they are. I only hope it will be for the better.'

Farewell to Moedling

It's July and the school holidays have begun. Yesterday Herbert and Ernsti and I were playing hide and seek in the garden. I went out into the road to see if I could find a place to hide, and then saw two boys looking at me through the fence of the back garden opposite. It was Weiss, who sits next to me in my class, and Rosenzweig, another Jewish boy in our class who has sometimes had the best exam results. I went over to them and asked what they were doing. They just looked at me, then Weiss said 'nothing – we are just talking', and I feel that they didn't want to talk to me, so I went back into our garden.

Today it's a beautiful morning. I am sitting on a bench in the Moedling railway station car park, waiting for Muttie's train to arrive in half an hour's time. It's almost six months since I waved goodbye to her, and I am really looking forward to seeing her again. And I am also looking forward to going to England and seeing Papa and Fred again. It will be quite strange me having to speak in English, and for Muttie as well, because she hasn't even learnt any at school. I wonder what my English granny is like, and what the house where we will be living is like.

I'll be going to an English school, and the English children won't know about what's been happening in Austria and Germany. I'll have to tell them about how everything will be changing now with the Nazis in power, and all the wonderful things they are doing in Germany, with everybody working together to make things better. There'll be Autobahns and Volkswagens and healthy holidays for all, not just a few. I shall tell them they should have National Socialism in England too.

As I am thinking about these things, a woman comes along and sits down at the far end of the bench I am sitting on. I look over at her, and it is Frau Doctor Loewe, the wife of our Doctor and the mother of Roland Loewe, Fred's friend. I haven't seen her for a while, but I think she should remember me because I had been in her flat with Fred to play with Roland. But she doesn't look at me, and I realise then she is talking to herself. I listen and realise she keeps on repeating the same thing. She is saying 'what can we do, what can we do'. She looks quite strange, like someone in a dream.

For a little while I take no notice, and just let her mumble on. I am trying to think what had happened. Perhaps her husband had died suddenly. Then I realise it might be something to do with Doctor Loewe not being allowed to treat non- Jewish patients any more. Perhaps it was affecting their income. Whatever it is, I feel I should say something, so I turn towards her and say 'don't worry, Frau Doctor, it'll be alright. Everything will get better'. She looks at me and seems to come to, like out of a dream. But she doesn't say anything, and just gets up and walks away.

Then I can see Muttie's train coming in, and walk over to the station. I feel upset about Frau Loewe, but good for having spoken to her. I really believe everything will be alright.

Part 2

The War – and What Followed

My childhood ended when I came to England. What follows describes my life in London during and immediately after the war, and my experiences then which have now, in my retirement, prompted me to unearth the facts about what they (i.e. the Germans and Austrians) knew about the gas chambers and the other atrocities committed by the Nazi Regime, and also what we, the British, knew about our bombing of German cities and the American bombing of Japanese cities..

This I have done with considerable help from historians, reporters, participants and victims of the war, making use of published material by them and other sources where necessary. Finally, I have added a tribute to those Germans and Austrians who, although not Jewish, were executed or perished in concentration camps because they failed to go along with what the Nazis believed in.

London – a new beginning

My youthful enthusiasm for Nazism abated soon after my taking up residence in England, and my parting words to Frau Loewe in the Moedling station park in July 1938, 'don't worry, it'll be alright – everything will get better', often came back to haunt me in later years.

When I first arrived in England I myself had been well on the way to becoming a committed Nazi, albeit in a juvenile way. Many of the people I respected and even admired in Austria had been Nazis, and being at an impressionable age, and in the absence of my parents, they became my role models. In addition, the whole scenario of National Socialism developing in Germany was one of healthy, energetic activity. There was no longer any unemployment – there were things to do for everybody. There were autobahns being built, the VW was already mooted as the new 'people's car which would become available to everybody. There was 'Strength through Joy' with active holidays for the young and there was the 'winter help' available to those at the bottom rung of the income ladder to help them over their most difficult time of the year. The German Army, the 'Wehrmacht', was disciplined, had smart uniforms, and was preparing to retrieve the territories stolen as a consequence of the punitive Treaty of Versailles. Shortly after the annexation we had heard the rhyme 'in Maerz (March) he makes a Scherz (joke – i.e. he annexes Austria), and in May he takes the Czechoslovakay', implying that all this was just the start. The Germans would once more take their rightful place in Europe. Even God was on their side, as implied by the Nazi motto 'For God, Fuehrer and Fatherland'.

As for the anti-Semitism, this was nothing new, and had been rampant throughout Europe for generations. Hitler only wanted to remove the Jews from positions where they could further communism and capitalism. He would see to it that they could go to their own lands, like Palestine, or perhaps settle them in Madagascar.

So where were my real loyalties? Of course the British were also an 'Aryan' nation, and in all probability would eventually be won over to National Socialism, and become a part of the Axis powers together with Italy. It was all quite inevitable in my childish mind.

My arrival in England with my mother was something of a shock. After leaving a Moedling bathed in sunshine and full of trees and greenery in its full summer splendour, we found ourselves in the London suburb of Sydenham which, though by London standards considered a green suburb, was mostly full of dull red-brown and grey brick houses made duller by a grey blanket of sky which showed no sign of lifting to admit the sun, and with a cool breeze wafting stray bits of newspapers across the roads.

Father together with Fred had already taken up residence at grandmother's boarding house in Sydenham. This turned out to be a substantial 3-story house dating back to the end of the 19th century, with a small front garden and a larger one behind the house incorporating some mature trees which helped to give it an air of privacy. Grandmother was welcoming and affectionate in her way, though hugging and kissing were not her forte. Mother had last seen her in Berlin in 1924 when grandmother and Winnie, father's sister, had come to stay with her and father in their flat. Granny and Winnie had both returned to England before I was born in October of that year because the basic food situation in Berlin had been so bad that father had difficulty providing for them. So this was the first time Granny had ever seen me, though she had seen my brother Fred as a baby.

Granny was of frail stature, in contrast to her personality, which was anything but frail, not surprising in view of her extensive experiences both of family and of travel. She bustled vigorously about her boarding house, which at the time only had two permanent guests, and when not otherwise occupied would be found having a smoke using a long elegant cigarette holder whilst perusing the Times newspaper. She prepared evening meals for her lodgers, and when she was finished in the kitchen she would listen to the radio or play bridge if she could drum up a quorum from the residents, one of whom was a young Irish woman working as a secretary in central London, the other a middle aged Irishman reputed to be a writer.

Granny came from an upper middle class family, but had parted company with her parents at the tender age of nineteen in order to elope with a German artist by the name of Buch. Her parents had not considered him to be a suitable husband for her, so she decided to marry the man she loved regardless, even though he was some twenty years older.

Peter Buch was a self-employed lithographic artist, not in what could be called regular employment. On his death certificate he was described as a 'journeyman artist'.

Though coming from a farming family in the vicinity of Frankfurt/Main, he had waved farewell to the soil and, after studying art at Heidelberg University, he embarked on an international artistic life. He managed to acquire customers both in London and Berlin, and during the good years he, grannie and the children, when the latter were not at school, would travel back and forth to rented accommodation in both cities. In later life one of his commissions had been to make a lithographic copy of a painting of Queen Victoria at Buckingham Palace on the occasion of her Golden Jubilee, though I never got to see this.

Peter Buch and his family were thus able to lead a varied and urbane life alternating between London and Berlin until the beginning of the First World War. They were living in Hackney at that time, and the general anti-German feeling probably led to a decline in his commissions. When he died of pneumonia in 1915, my aunt Ena, Winnie's sister, was convinced his death was also partly due to a broken heart at seeing the end of all his dreams for the future, and being parted from his only son who was then (probably, as far as he knew) already in the German Army..

The family's finances were now in dire straits, and grannie had to find employment in order to survive. She became housekeeper to Sir Charles Buxton, an Independent Labour MP and intellectual who boasted George Bernard Shaw amongst his friends. By that time grannie had changed the family name to Bush in order to avoid anti-German prejudice both against herself and the children at school. This Anglicised version of 'Buch' (i.e. German for 'Book) was also adopted by my father after the end of the war, meaning that I was born a Bush, and registered as such with the British Consulate in Berlin.

Our first few weeks at granny's were spent in getting used to the boarding house routines. Father and Fred both had jobs in London, father as bookkeeper for an Austrian Jewish Engineer refugee, and Fred as a dispatch assistant at the printers of the 'Picture Post' magazine. They took a train from Sydenham station early in the morning, so mother and I had time on our hands, except at weekends when we were on a round of visits to and from father's sisters Winnie and Ena with their husbands. In the evenings we all sat together in the communal lounge at the boarding house, the adults chatting or playing cards, and Fred and I reading a book. We had our first visit to an English cinema together, and this later became my Mecca, often resulting in weekly visits.

During the days I was occupied with swatting up on my school English, and practising what I learnt doing shopping errands for granny. I was still wearing my leather shorts, which attracted some attention in Sydenham High Street, though tempered by British reticence towards indulging in conversation with strangers, even children.. Granny had been taken aback by some very short white shorts I had worn on the first really hot days, since she considered that they looked too much like English underpants, and persuaded my father to stop me wearing them. I thought this was quite unreasonable at the time, since nobody in Moedling had ever been scandalized by them

I also tried to take granny's dog Bonzo, a cross between a bulldog and a terrier, for walks, but had to give in to Granny's procedure of letting him take his walks alone, which he did, often to the amusement of locals when he held up the traffic crossing Sydenham High Street at a leisurely pace, an exercise he would not have survived for long in today's traffic.

When not out and about providing a focus of interest in my leather shorts, I would spend a lot of time, at father's direction, preparing myself for my first term at Sydenham Central school by learning to understand the quaint British currency with its pounds, shillings and pence. For the sake of readers of a more tender age, I might just explain that each pound was worth twenty shillings, and each shilling twelve pence. In addition, inexplicably, there was the 'guinea', which, although no longer available as a coin, signified an amount of twenty one shillings, and was still used on legal transactions.

I believe Britain was the only European country not having a decimal currency at that time. The resistance to change and the adherence to tradition, both, as I later learnt, landmarks of the British character, made work for innumerable accountants and no doubt helped to denude our planet of its rain forests, which at that time was not a matter of public concern. A further brake on progress consisted of the stubborn adherence to measuring weights in pounds, stones and hundredweights (actually equivalent to one hundred and twelve pounds), all a nightmare for one used to just kilos and grams. Then there were Inches and feet, instead of centimetres and metres, miles instead of kilometres, and last but by no means least, degrees Fahrenheit instead of centigrade. So I had to learn all this and more, at the same time trying to read my first English books using the rudimentary knowledge of English acquired during my two years at the Moedling grammar school. Amongst other useful basics I had been taught there was this: when looking out of a train window in England, and a fellow passenger shouts 'look out', this is not meant to encourage you to stick you head further out of the window. On the contrary, it is simply a warning of impending danger, in this case of having it knocked off by a passing train if you do!

When not engaged in acquiring essential information about my new homeland, i.e. my Motherland (instead of my Fatherland, though in my case the latter term would have been more appropriate) I spent time in granny's large back garden, which by English standards would have been described as un-kempt, and also in a semi-basement garden workshop where I was able to make fretwork models of the Disney characters from 'Snow White and the Seven Dwarves', which had surfaced on European screens some while before.

My English studies were to prepare me to attend the local 'Central' school, which was somewhere between a secondary and a grammar school, and only about fifteen minutes' walk from Granny's house. It had the additional benefit of having Mr. Third, a remote relative, as headmaster. My initiation to the school was eased by his presence, and he was soon rewarded by my progress, particularly at English classes where my teacher was able to report my getting top marks in English grammar, obviously not a popular subject of study for my fellow pupils, though essential in my English and Latin studies at my previous school.

I also made some friends, who were all curious to hear my accounts of where I had come from. I enjoyed the relatively relaxed discipline at the school, and the fact that there was not the great gulf between teachers and pupils I had been accustomed to in Austria. It was, in addition, a novel experience to be fitted out with a school uniform, which was not a practice customary at my school in Austria. I was quite proud of my long grey flannel trousers, black coat and cap with the school badge. In addition to my top-of-the class performance in English Grammar I also did well in French, and was soon top of the class in art, where the young teacher was impressed by my sketching ability, possibly inherited from my grandfather.

A new experience for me was cricket, which was unknown in Austria. Although Sydenham Central school was not equipped with a sports field (in fact it had no more than a large asphalted playground, we were occasionally taken to a cricket field belonging to another school to enable us to become proficient at this national sport. On my second visit there I had been delegated to do 'fielding'. Not being particularly sports minded, my attention had strayed to a group of girls from another school who were passing by, when I was hit on the head by the ball I should have caught. It might have been this incident, repeating my head's unexpected contact with a ball first experienced at the football game in Berlin, but in the rather more concentrated and harder form of an English Cricket ball, which lead to my diminished interest in ball games thereafter.

My lack of enthusiasm for the national sport of my new homeland was fortunately balanced by my loss of enthusiasm for Nazism, together with any desire to spread its message, which was just as well as the political situation between Britain and Germany was becoming more strained at the time. Hitler's manoeuvres were definitely regarded as 'not cricket' by the British establishment, which was by then finding Oswald Mosley's blackshirts enough of an embarrassment. Since politics had never been discussed with us children at home, my parents were not aware of my thoughts in this connection, and took it for granted that I would imbibe British culture quickly, and thus repeat my father's experience of becoming German in Berlin in reverse by becoming British in London.

Father was planning for us to have our own flat in due course, but finances were not up to it at the time. The only alternative was for mother to become a wage earner as well, so after I started school she became a resident housekeeper to a local ex-patriate Swedish family. It was a difficult time for all of us, but particularly for mother, who had become used to having some domestic help of her own in our previous household, bolstered up by father's relatively comfortable income at that time. She was not happy with her employers either, and when I visited her there was the only time in my life I ever saw her cry.

Our social circumstances had thus changed drastically from those we had become used to in Moedling. We were no longer middle class with a circle of friends and acquaintances from the business community. Both father and mother must have felt bitterly disappointed by this change. Gone for good were their frequent outings and parties with friends, our regular family summer holidays together, meals out on Sundays after visits to the swimming pool, bridge parties and outings to the local wine cellars, night clubs and attendance at the New Year's Ball at the Hofburg Palace, not to mention mother's occasional visits to her relatives in Berlin.

Above all, our standing in society had taken a knock: we were now very much lower middle class. Neither father nor mother ever complained or indulged in self- pity. For my father this was probably a trait inherited from his 'journeyman artist' father, whose lifestyle had been adventurous, always living for the moment, never knowing what the future might hold in store.

If anything, it was worse for mother, who had actually had a working class upbringing. Her father had been a gilder, and after leaving school she was apprenticed to a milliner. Her eight years in Austria had been like a dream come true, even though throughout those years she had to work hard. Now she had to work harder, but without the rewards of a privileged lifestyle.

Once in England, I was subjected to a quite different scenario, and once again influenced by people I admired. Some, like the young woman who had been living at grandmother's boarding house and the young Communist who later became her husband, and his parents, also committed Communists, were regular guests in our new home. Due to their influence I quickly came to see the fallacies of National Socialism. My parents never knew how involved I had been with Nazism during my last few months in Moedling with the Krisch family. The one piece of evidence, the picture postcard I had sent to mother when she was in Berlin staying with her socialist brother, with the brief but telling question whether uncle Paul had changed his socialist views yet, was never mentioned by her. Presumably it either got lost in the post, or was censured by Nazi inspectors. Due to the reticence I inherited from my father, I was too embarrassed to ever raise the card with her at the time. It would have been tantamount to admitting to strong feelings, something both my parents tended to avoid.

The war

I remember well the day war was declared, September 3rd 1939. Chamberlain's speech announcing this, on a bright but hazy Sunday morning, was listened to by a very substantial part of the population. The streets in Sydenham, at any rate, were empty. To add drama to the situation, shortly after the speech the air raid sirens in Sydenham started up. It was the first time we had heard them performing in their true role, although there had been 'demonstration' alarms to familiarise us with the repetitive 'up-and-down' pitch of the 'warning', meaning enemy aircraft approaching, later followed by the continuous tone of the 'all clear', meaning enemy aircraft gone.

On this occasion, although there was no panic, we feared the worst. For what seemed like hours, but was in reality no more than a matter of a quarter of an hour, everybody in Sydenham was listening out for the sound of aircraft. Then the 'all clear' sounded. There was no radio announcement explaining what had happened, but we later heard it had just been 'a test'. In the event, as far as Londoners were concerned, the war in the air did not start for another six months.

By this time we were already in our little two-bedroom flat not very far from granny's boarding house. I had been given the choice of being evacuated with the school or continuing at its current location with a skeleton staff of teachers, with the entailed risk that my education would suffer. As with the previous occasion when I was faced with the possibility of being parted from my parents, I opted to stay with them. They were both happy with that decision, even though they couldn't predict what the likely hazards of staying in London were to be. Looking back in later years I often thought how lucky I had been to have this option compared with some of my Jewish school friends, where the alternative to parting company with their parents was certain hardship, and a possible ultimate fate not even dreamt of in their worst nightmares.

The tensions of family life in our new surroundings eased after we had moved into our flat, and mother had been able to get a position as non-resident part- time housekeeper with a German diplomat's widow who lived with her son in a large house with a big garden not very far away. It was an ideal solution to mother's situation, since she now had time to learn English whilst still being able to converse in German with her employer, who was a cultured woman of kindly disposition. In the meantime father had obtained employment as a wages clerk at Muirheads, a local engineering factory.

It was my mother's (and our) good fortune that she possessed a stoicism that was little short of heroic. She now had to make do with a kitchen which was little more than a screened-off end of a passage with a little window at the end looking on to the wall of the adjacent house. It contained a gas cooker, a china sink, a small metal kitchen table, a food storage cupboard (not a fridge), and a few other cupboards and shelves. We did have a bathroom, but the toilet was off the landing on the floor below and shared with our landlord's daughter and her husband.

In spite of the rationing introduced at the beginning of the war, we never felt deprived as far as food was concerned, because mother was an exceptional manager. Amongst other improvisations, she started using the milk which was about to go sour for cream cheese, flavoured with chives she grew on the windowsill, and onions from a small vegetable plot we had been allocated in the garden, later to be augmented by vegetables from our allotment nearby. We had hot dinners at weekends, sometimes even roast chicken, though in-between times it was more likely to be 'Spam', a processed meat loaf shipped to us in huge quantities from the United States to help feed us. Gone were the days of sauerkraut with black pudding fetched by Fred and me for the occasional celebratory evening meal, but we did sometimes have the traditional English fish and chips instead, though not picked up in containers we could swing over our head, but just wrapped in newspaper, which was the custom at the time. As the war progressed, father and I were pampered by being provided with a two course hot lunch at our factory canteen as well, allowing mother some respite from her cooking duties.

Our flat was heated by open fires fuelled by coal which had to be carried upstairs in buckets from an outside bunker in the garden three flights of stairs below, supplemented by electric radiant heaters when it got really cold. Refuse, including ash, again had to be carried down three flights of stairs.

Although father, Fred and I did some of the fetching and carrying, this never involved the shopping which mother considered her sole responsibility. The bathroom was a bonus for us, since we had never had one in our flat in Austria. It had a rather vicious gas-fired hot water boiler to heat the bath water, which had to be lit manually each time, always accompanied by an explosive ignition. Having a bath did help in getting us warmed up on really cold winter days, in addition to enabling father to develop his photographic enlargements in the tub, since photography was to become his principal hobby throughout the war.

I continued my schooling at Sydenham Central School. Although most of my school mates had been evacuated, the remnant were now taught by a skeleton staff consisting mainly of teachers who were already retired, together with some newly appointed younger ones. We carried on as before, the only difference being that we no longer had organised sports away from the school, and we always had to carry our gasmasks with us in their cardboard boxes with string carrying loops.

Father was concerned about my education, and suggested I sat a matriculation exam with the idea of continuing my engineering career at college. I, however, had different ideas, and with father's assistance got an apprenticeship at his factory, backed up by a part-time course in Mechanical Engineering at the South East London Polytechnic, about a half hour's cycle ride away from home.

Muirhead & Co, the company we were working for, was a family concern at that time engaged in building electro-mechanical equipment for use in conjunction with guns on warships. Combined with my part time attendance at South East London Polytechnic, I was now launched on my engineering career. At work I was engaged on the fitting and assembly of 'Balancers', a piece of equipment used on naval gun turrets, under the supervision of Mr Noakes, my 'section leader', a skilled engineering fitter foreman nearing retirement age, and Bob, his young assistant, who had had his own watchmaking business before the war. We shared a large assembly bench and an adjacent bench with a row of lathes and drills.

During these years both father and I cycled to work, usually separately, because I didn't want to be seen as 'a father's boy'. We had our midday meals in the factory canteen, although separately since he had his in the 'staff' canteen, and I in the general works canteen.

Life 'on the bench' proved to be a formative experience for me. The people I associated with, like Bob, who sat on the opposite side of the bench, were mostly in their late thirties or early forties, and had had their own business before starting 'war work' as an optional alternative to being drafted into the armed forces.

Bob, it turned out, liked sailing in his spare time. Although single, he was reputed to have 'a relationship' with the pretty female supervisor of the women machine operators in a section just around the corner from where we worked, and whom, it later transpired, he shared his sailing holidays with. On the rare occasions when she came around to have a word with him she had to be brief, because the male workers were prone to start chanting a refrain of what was apparently a well known ditty with the repeated refrain of 'tell me the old old story', which they did whenever there were any prolonged social male-female dialogues taking place in their vicinity. I never found out whether this practice was a unique one associated with our company, or universal in industry, and can only assume it was prompted by the jealousy of those men who had no interesting relationships in or outside marriage.

Another aspect of factory life was 'the union'. With one or two exceptions, the workers in our department belonged to it, and our 'shop steward' came around to collect our 'subs' regularly. Our working conditions were, however, exceptional, and I don't recall any major management/worker disputes, possibly because the family owning the company were not required to compete in the market place since they were working on a government contract. They were also known to have a benevolent attitude to their employees, and a son of the family actually worked in the development laboratory. Nevertheless, our shop steward kept a sharp eye on things. A well-groomed man of middle age with Mephistophelian features, he was known to be a Communist, and once or twice invited me to attend union branch meetings, possibly hoping to make me a convert to his own belief. In addition to being a thorn in the side of the department manager, he lost no opportunity to discomfit an older man who had refused to become a union member by making fun of some of his fussy mannerisms. It was this activity more than anything which dissuaded me from having anything to do with him outside the company.

After the British evacuation from Dunkirk in June 1940 the war in the air had started in earnest. There were constant air raids on most days. The numerous barrage balloons which had become a feature of our lives, tethered in parks and open spaces throughout London, prevented low level bombing raids. We would often watch the German bombers being harassed and shot down by British fighter planes such as Spitfires and Hurricanes during this time, which was later to become known as 'The Battle of Britain.'

After three months of this, without any signs of Britain being prepared to capitulate, Hitler abandoned the idea of an invasion, which would have been disastrous without air supremacy, and all subsequent air attacks were carried out at night in order to avoid harassment by British fighters.

This change in German policy had a deleterious effect on my evening class attendance, since the raids often started before I could get home, and since my only method of transport consisted of a bicycle, I was exposed to the shrapnel from our anti-aircraft shells. I eventually wore an army helmet to lessen the danger of being injured, and in the event I wasn't hit once. However, as a result of the change from daytime to night-time air raids the College eventually adopted the simple expedient of transferring the evening to week end classes, which meant that my Saturdays and Sundays were largely taken up by these.

Partly due to the black-out and the increasing hazards of going out when the regular night-time air raids were in progress in the latter years of the war, the radio had become a major source of home entertainment. Evenings at home were therefore often spent listening to programmes such as ITMA (acronym for 'It's that man again'), a comedy radio programme featuring the comedian Tommy Handley, or 'the Brains Trust' consisting of a panel of four well-known personalities answering listeners' questions, sometimes including my idols J.B. Priestley and Bertrand Russell.

An additional source of entertainment was provided by the German propaganda station featuring a commentator who had acquired the nick-name 'Lord Haw-haw' from his British audience, due to his somewhat stilted upper-class accent. For the most part his obvious exaggerations about the extent of German military successes and the devastation caused by Luftwaffe raids did not appear to cause the British Ministry of Propaganda serious concern.

What was not so well known to the British public, but to us as German- speakers, was the British response to Lord Haw-haw provided by 'Soldaten sender Calais' (Soldier Station Calais), broadcast in German from Sussex and aimed at the Wehrmacht occupation troops in France. After accidentally hitting on this station, father often tuned in to it for light entertainment. Although giving every appearance of an official Wehrmacht station it was peppering its generally factual statements with just sufficient misinformation to shake the German soldiers' faith in their leadership. In addition the programmes played a lot of American swing and even jazz, both apparently popular with the rank and file of the Wehrmacht but frowned on by the Nazi elite.

By this time Fred was already conscripted into the Royal Air Force Regiment, and I had joined the Air Training Corps. This meant I had to spend a couple of evenings a week being instructed in air navigation, maths, weaponry and marching routines by various adult volunteers with experience of these subjects to prepare us for service in the Royal Air Force.

In spite of retaining a slight accent, I never experienced any problems associated with my German origins either at work or in the ATC. Mother, however, was occasionally the subject of furtive glances and comments in the wartime queues for food in view of her pronounced German accent, a problem father did not encounter because of his English up-bringing. However, he later joined the Home Guard, and when it became known to his commanding officer that he had fought on the other side in the previous war he was asked to resign and had to hand back his uniform. It was a bitter blow to him, particularly after having at last been able to belong to a group with common aims in the country he was born in. As always he bore his misfortune with humour and resignation.

After the initial handiwork entailed in providing black-out screens for our windows, a statutory requirement policed by the local voluntary air-raid wardens, father's spare time was taken up by other pressing activities he had not been familiar with in his previous life. The most important of these was taking on an allotment to grow vegetables to supplement our diet. Then there was the maintenance of his bicycle which had become his principal mode of transport to and from Muirhead & Co. This entailed a return journey of some 5 miles each way in all weathers, often returning in the black-out without any street lighting.

The remainder of his spare time was then devoted to his previous hobbies from our Austrian days of keeping an aquarium of tropical fish, together with his continuing life-time hobby of photography.

As a member of the Air Training Corps, I was subjected to repeated Air Crew Selection tests conducted by the Royal Air Force in connection with my volunteering for air crew duties. In the event, I never succeeded in becoming part of the top five per cent of applicants creamed off from what was by that time a surfeit of volunteers. My lack of success may have been inadvertently my own doing, since during the interviews with the examiners, and following their usual eyebrow raising when they noted I was born in Berlin and still had a slight German accent, I always answered the question as to why I was volunteering for aircrew duties candidly with the statement 'I have always wanted to learn to fly'.

This was probably not the sort of answer that would have gone down well at the time. I was, however, not foolish enough to mention I had German relatives, since even to my naïve mind at the time it was obvious that this would have resulted in my being moved further down the list. Strangely, the thought that I might one day be called upon to drop bombs on my extended German family in Berlin never occurred to me, possibly because I felt that the likelihood of that happening was so remote.

However, volunteering for aircrew training did, with hindsight, have its plus points. The first one was not one I would have regarded as such at the time, but in post-war years I realised I couldn't have chosen a better way of avoiding active combat. The second one was the privilege of having a white band inserted into the turn-ups of the smart forage caps of our ATC uniforms, which of course gave us a certain kudos amongst the public in general and any likely girlfriends. The latter, however, failed to materialise in my case due to my excessive shyness.

So I and others ended up remaining safely on the ground, apart from a few week-end flights as passenger with fellow ATC cadets in smaller transport planes to acquaint us with the medium of our choice. In addition I continued my ATC activities by learning more about astronavigation and trigonometry which I enjoyed. Other training such as rifle maintenance and parade-ground drilling was of less interest to me. The latter activity consisted of marching in step with about thirty other boys and carrying out a number of manoeuvres to instructions bellowed out by a diminutive ex-army sergeant major. His bellicose and vociferous commands were in contradiction to a kindly and forgiving nature, often severely tried by my inability to concentrate on what I considered the brainless tasks involved. On occasion I caused some havoc on parade by this lack of concentration, such as continuing to march straight on when the rest were attempting a right or left-wheel in accordance with the bellowed commands.

Looking back, our most hazardous experience of the war was having a 250 lb bomb fall into the front garden of the house next door, with a crater deep enough to sink a car in, but causing no injuries and little damage to this house nor the adjacent ones apart from broken windows. After that there was a spate of incendiary bombs which I was allowed to assist in extinguishing by bringing along buckets of sand. Later on during the continuing night raids, a landmine dropped on to our local department store just about a quarter of a mile from our flat. The store was razed it to the ground, but nobody was hurt, and for the remainder of the war our luck held out. The East End of London including the docks area, however, was not so lucky, and the civilian casualty lists there were considerable

After the raids on the London Docklands had started, father heard that the offices of the publisher to whom he had sent a copy of his book entitled *A Son of two Nations* had been destroyed by fire. Although it must have been an additional blow for him, I think he had by then accepted that there was little hope of it being accepted by any publisher at that time, and shortly after the war he destroyed his remaining copy because, on re-reading it, he had decided it was too amateurish.

Before the German air raids started Fred and I had helped the Langshaws, the family who owned the house and lived in the flats below us, to install an 'Anderson' air-raid shelter in the garden. This simply consisted of some corrugated steel panels curved and bolted together at the top, lowered into a rectangular hole dug as deep as we could get it into the ground, with the earth dug out heaped up around the sides projecting above ground.

When the first Battle of Britain events took place in the skies above us we spent more time outside the shelter than inside, watching the German bombers being harassed by British fighter planes, at least until the first bombs landed just about a mile away. Only later, when the night raids started, did we all spend nights together in the shelter. Even this didn't last long, since the discomfort of seven of us in close proximity in the shelter proved too much, and we all decided to take the risk of staying indoors instead. Being up on the third floor we did feel more vulnerable, but our landlord had made it clear that we would be welcome to keep them company in their basement kitchen whenever the night time raids came too close for comfort.

Our landlord's family were exceptionally friendly and helpful towards us, and did much to strengthen my loyalties to my English motherland. Helped by a copious amount of time spent reading history and philosophy books from the local library, my political orientation had quickly changed from National Socialism to Socialism, and I now became a Socialist, i.e. one of those I had contemptuously referred to as 'Sozis' in Austria.

Driven by my left-wing ideals at that time I had attended a so called 'second front' meeting in Trafalgar Square in 1942 addressed by Aneurin Bevan, the Labour MP, amongst others. This meeting had been organised by the Communist Party, who claimed that Britain's failure to open a second front against the Germans in Europe was driven by the conservative element in the coalition, led by Winston Churchill, wanting to hold back until the Germans had finished off Russia, or vice versa. Churchill was infuriated and referred to Aneurin Bevan as 'that squalid nuisance' afterwards. Little did he dream at the time that this squalid nuisance was destined to become a Minister in the next government, and in addition the prime mover behind the setting up of Britain's National Health Service. When the Second Front finally started in Normandy at the beginning of June 1944, it came about mainly due to pressure from the Americans, who overrode Churchill's views that it would result in a catastrophic failure.

Not long after it started, I was looking out of my bedroom window late one evening on hearing what sounded like a powerful motorcycle in the distance. Since the window was on the third floor I could see out across Kent and towards the Thames Estuary, and the origin of the sound appeared to be a plane with an engine on fire. Then the sound stopped, the plane nose-dived and I heard the thud of an explosion. It wasn't until the following day, after several repeats of this happening that I realised that what I had seen was not an aircraft on fire, but some kind of German missile. Another week elapsed before the government released information about the V1, the German secret weapon (the 'V' standing for 'Vergeltung', meaning 'revenge', presumably for the Allied bombing of German cities). Later named 'the doodlebug' because of the similarity of the sound it produced to a Scottish bag-pipe, it was arriving over London in increasing numbers, and causing considerable damage with its 1000lb of explosive content.

Since the doodlebugs came over at a relatively low height, it was actually possible to take evasive action if seen from a distance, and for that reason alone they caused continuous disturbance in our everyday lives. On one occasion mother had to run for it, being chased by a doodlebug coming the street at the market where she was shopping. She managed to get away from its line of travel before it dropped and exploded out of her sight. Another even more un-nerving feature of the doodlebug was caused by an un-planned design malfunctioning of its propulsion unit. This occurred when the fuel, instead of being ignited intermittently in the propulsion jet tube, starting to burnt continuously, still giving sufficient thrust for the doodlebug to glide down soundlessly before hitting the ground and exploding.

During the initial stages of the V1 attacks we were ordered into the air raid shelters at the factory as soon as they were spotted heading in our general direction at the coastal observation stations.. After a while it was realised that this was causing a virtual cessation of production, so they had an observer on the roof who would signal if he saw a V1 coming right towards us, and we would then merely take cover underneath our benches.

Since the means of targeting the doodlebugs relied simply on orienting them with a directional control and determining their range by means of a rudimentary device which cut off the fuel after the V1 had travelled a pre-set distance, their targeting accuracy was negligible. Although a considerable number landed in the Greater London area, any idea of reaching 'strategic' targets had obviously been abandoned. In addition to this, on a number of occasions I witnessed V1s flying around in a circle after having part of one wing sliced or damaged by barrage balloon cables, or damaged by anti-aircraft fire or a pursuing fighter plane.

With the continuing advance of the Allies across mainland Europe, some of the main launching pads of the V1 were eliminated, but the Germans then continued using mobile launch pads. Soon, however, another missile known as the V2 started to arrive. These were simply rockets, again carrying around 1000lb of explosive, pre-targeted by orientating their flight path and metering the amount of rocket fuel. Their accuracy was, if anything, less than that of the V1s. A feature overlooked by the Germans was that since there was no warning of their impending arrival, the effect on morale of the V2s was less than that of the V1s. In fact, since they landed at supersonic speeds, even the sound of their approach was not heard until after they exploded. Not long after they started, a V2 came down in a field next to our factory. It killed a cow, and provided lunchtime entertainment for me in collecting some of the copper remains of the missile strewn around.

As the war progressed, public opinion in Great Britain had become increasingly influenced by propaganda, and there was a growing body of opinion that it was not just Nazism we were up against, but some ingrown racial trait of the Germans. They were now called 'the Hun' by Churchill, 'the Boche' by Air Chief Marshall 'bomber Harris', and as 'the Jerry' by the general populace. The term 'Hun' had already been used as a derogatory term for Germans during the first world war, and was based on an address by Kaiser Wilhelm in 1902 to German troops being shipped to China to deal with the Boxer Rebellion there. The Kaiser had used the term in the context of exhorting his troops to emulate the Huns under Attila and take no prisoners.

Although mother seldom made any comments on politics or indeed her own feelings about the life we were now leading compared with the one we had led in Austria, she must have found all this profoundly difficult to come to terms with. She had, after all, a father and two brothers with their families living in Berlin at the time, and had lost all contact with them after the beginning of the war. Her only consolation in those years was her friendship with two German women married to British husbands who lived in the vicinity, together with some other sympathetic friends, most notably Kathleen, the Irish girl who had been a lodger at Granny's boarding house and was now married to a young RAF Pilot Officer with a strong Communist background.

Later on during the war father became a member of what was, somewhat ill-advisedly, named the 'Common Wealth' party, since it was not in any sense meant to be associated with the British Commonwealth, but with the idea of 'common wealth', i.e. sharing the nation's natural and industrial resources for the 'common good'. The party was formed by the one- time Liberal MP Sir Richard Acland and his wife, who were both teachers, and had the initial though short-lived backing of the writer J.B. Priestly. Its idealistic message was based on the underlying idea of applying Christian principles to politics by creating the maximum well-being for the greatest number. Its principal difference from what was then the policy of the Labour party which was in the war-time coalition with the Conservative and Liberal parties, was that it was driven by rather more idealistic motives. Its aim of putting an upper limit on incomes made it into a left-wing 'ginger' group with a Christian motif.

Following father's lead, I joined and became the local branch's treasurer at the tender age of twenty, with him being the Secretary and Chair. We had regular branch meetings in our little flat with the other members, who never exceeded six in number, at least one of whom happened to be a friend of father's who joined more out of friendship than conviction.

Mother remained on the side-lines, and never participated in the meetings, conditioned no doubt by her German upbringing, where politics were an exclusively male domain, which she was content to leave to her husband and male offspring. She merely provided sustenance for us and the visiting party members, which she did extremely well looking back, bearing in mind the rationing and prevalent food shortage.

Towards the end of the war, early in 1945, I took a decision which was influenced by reports of the indiscriminate bombing of German cities coupled with my extensive reading in philosophy and politics, and decided I could no longer support what we were doing in Europe. I therefore prepared to report to the local government office to register as a conscientious objector.

Father tried to talk me out of it, and eventually got me to have a word with my ATC commanding officer who lived just down the road from us. He was a very mild mannered and sympathetic man, and tried his best to dissuade me on the basis of purely practical considerations, such as that the end of the war was in sight, and anything I might decide to do would not make any difference. Being the determined and obstinate person I was, however, I regarded it as a matter of principle, and the following day set off on my bike for the appropriate local government office.

Luckily, it was closed. This might have been one of those coincidences of history which has a profound effect on our subsequent lives, though I doubt whether it would have caused anything more than head-scratching at the local council offices. In the event, It gave me just the extra time I needed for further reflection. I then changed my mind, having come to the conclusion that my action in terms of the practicalities involved would be regarded as little short of laughable by those in authority and indeed by my family, friends and fellow workers at the factory. After all, apart from being an ATC aircrew volunteer, my only connection with the war at the time was being in a ‘reserved occupation’, meaning I was engaged in doing war work in a factory. I therefore abandoned my principles mainly because I couldn’t face making myself look ridiculous.

When the war ended, the first reports about what had been discovered at the extermination camps in Poland were made public. Although mother never once commented about what she read in the papers or heard on the news, I believe her initial reaction was that it was all just anti-German propaganda. I don't think she or father at that stage fully believed in the Holocaust. I myself found it difficult to come to terms with, and often wondered what had happened to my Jewish classmates at the Grammar school in Moedling.

At the general elections which took place immediately after the end of the war, the Commonwealth Party fielded a couple of parliamentary candidates, and I volunteered to do some canvassing on their behalf. This involved a bus and train journey to the constituency of Wing Commander Millington, one of our candidates. Looking back now, I am still impressed by the friendly reception I experienced from many of the households I dropped leaflets to. All of twenty years old, I didn't look older than seventeen at the most, and was only driven to this activity which involved having to communicate with strangers by my passionate zeal for the cause. My German accent would have been noticeable, yet. I didn't experience a single rebuff, even from people who, judging by the houses they occupied and their demeanour, were most likely Conservatives. Undoubtedly their friendly response was mainly due to my obvious immaturity, but it went some way towards reinforcing my feeling of belonging.

This feeling was further strengthened when Wing Commander Millington was elected, which proved that I had played a miniscule part in the defeat of the Conservative Party, resulting in the replacement of Churchill by Attlee, the new Labour Party prime minister. It was a major political upheaval, and caused worldwide astonishment at the ingratitude of the British people to the man under whose leadership they had defeated Hitler. According to the Conservative party and other Churchill supporters, it wasn't the British people but the British working class that was to blame, which at the time reinforced another 'belonging' for me – i.e. to the working class!

With my friends Walter on the left and Herbert on the right in Moedling in 1948

Posing with Herbert alongside a poster of Stalin put up outside the Foersterhaus Inn in Moedling 1948

Walter's father when he was Chief Engineer at the Moedling Municipal Baths in 1938

Herbert's father after he joined the Wehrmacht in 1942

The Weber family before Theresienstadt

Lans von Liebenfels as a Catholic Novice

The Downfall

So how was it that Germany and later Austria, both one time democracies which had been among the world leaders in contributions to literature, the arts and sciences, could, within six years, become pariahs to the rest of the world?

There were two contributory factors common to the speedy collapse of the democratic governments of both Germany and Austria – poverty and unemployment. In both countries extreme wings of the political spectrum had formed their own armed gangs that roamed the streets and engaged in breaking up each other's public meetings. In the 1932 elections following the financial collapse of the Weimar Republic in Germany, the National Socialists polled some 33% of the votes (a drastic improvement over the 2.6% they polled in 1928). This was more than their nearest rival, the Socialists, although combined with the Communists they could muster 38%. After two failed attempts at forming a coalition with the Nazis, the right wing German National party supported the nomination of Hitler as Chancellor, regarding his appointment as a purely temporary measure. They had completely underestimated the rabid nature of the National Socialists, and. within weeks of becoming chancellor Hitler had established control by getting his Storm Troopers to arrest all known Communist and Socialist party officials. They were quickly dispatched to the nearest concentration camps already set up for this purpose.

Faced with imminent threats to their own liberty, and the growing popularity of the Nazis with their promises of full employment and 'Winter Help' for the needy, the right wing establishment then decided to take the easy course of 'going with the flow'.

In the case of Austria, the downfall came in March 1938, five years into the Nazi regime in Germany. Hitler had issued an ultimatum to Schuschnigg, the Austrian Chancellor at the time, that he should immediately appoint Seiss Inquart from the Austrian Nazi party to the position of Interior Minister, followed by a plebiscite on the question of unification with the Reich.

When Schuschnigg ignored Hitler's demand, the Wehrmacht invaded, and were welcomed by the great majority of the population. At the subsequent plebiscite arranged by Hitler over 98% voted for unification with the Reich. Even allowing for a considerable amount of intimidation at the polling booths, and the fact that neither Jews, representing some 4% of the population, nor Gypsies, were allowed to vote, this was still a surprising result. After all, at the last previous parliamentary elections in 1930, i.e. eight years before, the Social Democrats were the largest single party, having polled 41% of the votes.

This swing came after years of continuous in-fighting between the Social Democrats (the Sozis), the Communists (the Reds), the Fascist- cum- Catholic Christian Democrats (the Blacks) and the National Socialists (the Nazis).The economy was suffering from chronic mass unemployment and associated mass poverty. Its most likely explanation is that by 1938 most Social Democrats had changed their allegiance simply because they were led to believe that Hitler's Socialism was not that different from theirs. Furthermore, he had already succeeded in virtually eliminating unemployment in Germany. In addition, Jews dominated business and finance in Austria at a time when the gap between the richest and the poorest had reached crisis point, thus re-fuelling what had been a stagnant anti-Semitism since the middle ages.

Throughout history the Jews had held a special position in both Christian and Islamic countries for the simple reason that theirs was the only religion that did not forbid the lending of money against interest – one of the founding stones of capitalism. No wonder that they acquired considerable skills in this activity, so that by the time the Christian countries had relaxed their prohibition of money lending and accepted banking as a legitimate business, the Jews were disproportionally engaged in this.

The scenario of Jews amassing wealth and power to guard against hard times and the coming of the next pogrom is a scenario well illustrated by Lion Feuchtwanger's novel *Jud Suess (Jew Suess)*, which was made into films both by Hollywood in the Twenties and the Nazis in the Thirties, though with completely different interpretations. The Hollywood version portrayed the figure of Jew Suess as a tragic victim, the Nazi version as an evil schemer.

A unique feature of the Austrian situation which distinguished it from the German was that Austria's population not only included Jews but also Hungarians, Czechs, Poles and Serbo-Croats amongst others inherited from its Austro-Hungarian Empire days, none of whom would have been enthusiastic about the Nazi racial theories.

Austria had been a democracy from 1920 to 1932, when the Austro-Fascists under Dollfuss dissolved parliament. During those years it could boast of having contributed some of the leading writers, artists, musicians, and scientists of the 20th century, such as Zweig, Klimt, Mahler, Freud and Meitner, most of whom were Jews and became immediate targets of Nazi hate propaganda after the annexation.

Stefan Zweig, one of the first of the leading Austrian Jewish intellectuals to realise what was in store for them, had already left Austria voluntarily in 1934. A pan-European for many years, he could see the way the wind was blowing ahead of the rest. After six years residence in Britain he eventually settled in Brazil with his second wife. Although he came to love Brazil, the burden of his lost past together with everything he had stood for became too great. In 1942, he committed suicide together with his wife. As one of the world's most widely read authors of the nineteen twenties and thirties, his action appears to be inappropriate. But it does signify Zweig's total despair at seeing everything he had worked for most of his life being trodden underfoot. His epitaph, *The World of Yesterday*[21], is an account of what brought him to his early death. In the message he left behind, he refers to his despair at the loss of the bulk of his European readership, since his books were now banned throughout Germany and the German occupied part of Europe. His spiritual home had been ransacked by the Nazis. Perhaps he was lucky to have departed from this life without having to experience the full horror of what came later.

The simplest and therefore possibly the most widely accepted explanation for the downfall of Germany was that there was something inherent in its culture which inclined Germans to obedience and discipline at any cost, with a fanatical disposition to 'maintain order'. The fact that in this instance 'the new order' was aimed at enforcing the superiority of the Aryan race was not seen as going against their basic Christian tenets. On the contrary, as Hitler had explained to them, it was their duty to God to spread and enforce their superior civilization. Just as Richard Dawkins's selfish gene works ceaselessly to ensure the survival of the fittest, the Nazis were going to work ceaselessly to ensure the dominance of the Aryan race.

Finally persuading the Germans to go to war had not been easy. As William Shirer, the American journalist living in Berlin until America entered the war in 1942 describes in his *The Rise and Fall of the Thrid Reich*[22], the people in the streets of Berlin were apathetic and dazed to find themselves at war with Poland, even though Goebbels had concocted a scenario of an attack by Polish troops on a German border post

There was certainly none of the enthusiasm which had accompanied the declaration of the first world war. Although it had been on Hitler's agenda from the start, it was only made possible by the ceaseless work of his faithful propagandist Goebbels, who had hammered home the brutal unfairness of the treaty of Versailles, which had separated the industrial Ruhr from Germany and imposed crippling reparations. Any doubts of the German establishment about his aggressive policies had been quelled by the bloodless re-occupation of the Rhineland, followed by the annexation of Austria, then by the bloodless acquisition of parts of Czechoslovakia. Now it was the turn of Poland, followed by the Netherlands, Belgium, and finally France in quick succession. It was only after the first reverses on the Russian front that those Germans who had opposed these military adventures from the start were vindicated. But by that time the SS and Gestapo had gained a stranglehold over any possible opposition, and the Special SS 'Einsatz Gruppen' started their work 'cleansing' the local populations of Jews, gypsies and communist functionaries behind the front lines in Russia. As already mentioned, with some exceptions these atrocities were not committed by the Wehrmacht but by special units sworn to secrecy. The willing perpetrators formed a small minority, the great majority just going along with it to ensure their own survival.

Just one of numerous examples supporting this explanation is provided by the Austrian Chancellor Schuschniggs account of his imprisonment, first in Vienna and later in an assortment of concentration camps until the end of the war. He states that most of his guards, whether SS or Gestapo, disliked those who treated him with brutality. But they never raised any objections, because they well knew the likely consequences. Schuschnigg survived seven years of life in Sachsenhausen and Dachau concentration camps, and was even allowed visits from his wife, during one of which she conceived his second son.

Another account of life in a concentration camp by the Viennese Psychiatrist Victor Frankl in his book 'Man's search for meaning' arrives at the conclusion that neither being a prisoner nor a guard could tell you anything about where they stood in the scale of good versus evil. After the liberation of his camp by the Americans, some Jewish prisoners hid the camp commander from them until they agreed not to harm him. It was later found that this man had used some of his own money to purchase medicines for the prisoners.

The downfall of both Germany and Austria, both democracies before the event, can best be graphically portrayed by regarding the state as a colossal rock balanced on one edge and held in equilibrium by opposing sectors of its population, basically the Right and the Left of the political spectrum. When, due to accidents of history, one sector gains too much leverage, the state keels over and crushes the other sector. Those on top find themselves in absolute control virtually overnight, giving the deranged and criminal elements amongst them free range.

This explanation can be used for both the communist and the national socialist revolutions, which both accounted for untold sufferings of their victims. To ascribe the resulting evils to any one class or any one race is an understandable prejudice of the victims but not a rational assessment.

A return to Moedling

So now, with the war in Europe finished, and having become anglicised to at least a degree of 'belonging', though always with the reservation that I also had German roots, I had to cope with the facts of the Holocaust. Would any of the people I had admired and followed, at least in spirit, or any of my German relatives, for that matter, ever have had a hand in this? If not, how much had they known about what was going on at Auschwitz and the other 'Final Solution' camps?

Whatever ones views on this topic, there had never been any public statement or propaganda concerning a 'final solution', and anybody persistent enough to scan the boring and repetitive rants of 'Mein Kampf' for this would have had to admit that they had wasted their time. It contains, of course, innumerable diatribes against the Jews, with the author accusing them of being warmongers, prime movers of the scourges of capitalism, bolshevism, anarchism, atheism, degenerate art etc. but offers no suggestion on how to deal with them other than removing them from positions of authority and encouraging them to leave the Reich for another homeland. Indeed, if he had even as much as mooted forced emigration in 'Mein Kampf', it is unlikely he would ever have come to power.

Certainly the Krystallnacht,(the smashing of windows of synagogues and Jewish owned shops and buildings) which went back to the time just after I had left Moedling, was found to have generated so much unease amongst the German people in general and their religious communities in particular that the Nazi leadership was persuaded that such a tactic should never again be used.

In the summer of 1948 I returned to Moedling. My first meeting with Walter and Herbert in the ruins of the Vienna South station is engraved like a landmark in my memory. Here I was, a relatively well-off English tourist, meeting friends I had not seen for ten years, and who had actually participated in the war, even if only for a short time. The portrait taken of us together shortly after our first re-union shows how their war experiences in the interim coupled with the chronic food shortages had aged them to look years older than me.

My journey just three years after the end of the war to a country occupied by the four victorious allies had been made possible by my appointment as a draughtsman at the National Gas Turbine Establishment since 1946, followed by promotion to Assistant Experimental Officer Grade. This grand title, in spite of the 'officer' adjunct, had no military connotations whatsoever. It did, however, provide me with an opportunity of some casual conversations with one of three German scientists who had been 'commandeered' after the war to work at the establishment. However, these friendly chats (sometimes lapsing from English into German) did not go as far as enabling me to enquire whether he had known anything about the Holocaust. He was, in any case, a very pleasant cultured man, not at all the sort of person one could remotely associate with any inhuman acts.

By this time my parents had established that all our relatives, including my three cousins, had survived the war, as had all their Austrian friends. Having also established that my friends Herbert and Walter were now living in Vienna, I had arranged to spend my two weeks annual summer holidays with them, and since they had already planned a week's sailing holiday together with other friends in St.Wolfgang during the second week of my stay, I had agreed to also go there with them.

Vienna was now an international zone of the occupying powers, i.e. Russia, France, USA and Britain, within Lower Austria, which was occupied by the Russians. Moedling was actually in the Russian zone. A visit there, I had been informed by the Foreign Office, would require a special Visa from the Russian Occupation Authority, with uncertain prospects of success. I was therefore prepared to take a chance of not being permitted to visit Moedling itself, and just meet my friends in Vienna.

My journey by train to Vienna had to be convoluted, since the only permitted access to the International Zone of Vienna through the Russian Zone by train coming from France had to be via Villach in the South. There I had to change trains and get on to the Vienna Express from Rome, which was so full that I had to endure a whole night standing in the corridor. This trial was made worse by a rather unpleasant smell pervading the train, which I later learnt from my friends was due to the fact that most Austrians living in urban areas had been existing on a diet consisting principally of tinned beans since the end of the war.

After our first meeting on the remains of the platform of the Vienna South Station we took a taxi to my Hotel in the International Zone. There they left me to catch up with some sleep after we had made arrangements for dinner together that evening. As an international tourist, I was able to eat at the hotel, and entertain guests, without having to produce any ration cards. It soon became apparent that Herbert and Walter were overwhelmed by the surfeit of goulash and dumplings served, and succeeded in dealing with everything on offer speedily. Food shortage had evidently played a large part in their lives, and here they had a unique opportunity of a temporary respite, which I as a relatively wealthy British tourist was able to provide.

The evening was taken up with telling each other about our wartime experiences. Both Walter and Herbert had been conscripted towards the end of the war, and were eventually involved in the rearguard action against the Allies in France. Walter was taken prisoner by the Americans, and subsequently had a relatively easy time, since he got on well with his captors, and managed to get a position as bartender in the American Canteen of the camp he was in. Herbert, on the other hand, had a rough time in French captivity, and developed epilepsy as a result of being struck on the head with a rifle butt. After their release they both managed to be admitted to the University in Vienna, though in Walter's case there was some delay because he had to obtain special clearance since he had been conscripted into the Waffen SS. However, the fact that his father was known to have been a Social Democrat all his life persuaded the authorities to permit him to commence his veterinary studies at the University.

The question of the necessary visa required from the Russian authorities to make my visit to Moedling possible was dismissed by my friends as being unimportant. They both well knew that the Russians made no more than occasional spot-checks at the numerous crossing points from the international into the Russian Zones, and if there should be a problem my British Passport would simply result in my being directed to return to the International Zone. I trusted their judgment implicitly, and even if I hadn't, would have been reluctant to object and thereby admit my timidity to my already worldly- wise friends.

So the following day Herbert and Walter met me at the hotel, and we set off for Moedling together. After boarding the tram my friends pointed me to the only vacant seat, which happened to be next to a Russian soldier carrying a Kalashnikov, which seemed a rather unnecessary piece of equipment in this situation. My friends later told me that these weapons were occasionally used by their owners to persuade uncooperative women to submit to rape.

Moedling hadn't changed much in ten years, even though there was still some evidence of wartime bombardment. We went straight away to see Walter's parents at their flat at the Moedling Swimming Baths, which I well remembered from my pre-war visits. Walter's parents looked well, though Frau Kainrath had lost some weight in the current food situation. Herr Kainrath lost no time in showing me his Trades Union newspaper, just to affirm that he was still a Socialist. He hadn't changed much from when I last saw him, even though he was now manager of the baths.

Frau Kainrath rustled up a meal of macaroni for us all, which I felt embarrassed about under the circumstances where I as a visitor was living off the fat of the land in my hotel, a fact Walter couldn't resist informing his parents about.

Our next port of call was Fraeulein Anna, who still lived next to Spechtgasse 10, which had been my home. She was delighted and at the same time tearful to see me, and gave me a hug, which would have been regarded as too familiar in the old days. She told me right away that Fraeulein Tomanek was not at home, she was now training to be a Doctor in Innsbruck, and her house was occupied by the Russians. She qualified this, perhaps to soften the blow, by saying they were Officers. She also told me in a subdued voice about the things they had had to endure with the Russians in the town, and how some of them were fresh from the Russian steppes, and thought a WC was somewhere to wash your hands. She also said how all unattached women were in danger of being raped, as she had been.

I left her standing tearfully at her garden gate with a box of chocolates I had picked up for her in Vienna, and which apparently was quite a rarity in Moedling, whilst I cast a quick eye over what had been my home for over eight years. It was looking somewhat neglected, and there was no sign of its Russian occupants.

Walter later confirmed that, after the initial wave during the Russian occupation, rape was still prevalent in the Russian Zone, and no woman dared go out alone after dark. The local papers were not allowed by the Russian authorities to report incidents of rape other than by referring to 'an unknown' attacking a woman, 'unknown' in this case being the then accepted code for 'Russian soldier'.

The three of us then did a short walk up into the woods to remind us of the days when we played Old Shatterhand and the Apaches there. On the way back down, we stopped at the Kobenzl Inn terrace to take photos of us in front of a large poster of Stalin. We also stopped to have a look at where I had lived with Herbert and his family in 1938. Their flat was now occupied by someone else, since Frau Krisch had escaped to the American Zone at Salzburg, where she now lived with Herbert's father in a refugee camp.

We talked about Weiss and our other Jewish classmates. Neither Walter nor Herbert knew what had happened to them, but they believed they left Austria shortly after the Anschluss, as did most of the Jewish professional families, but they had no idea where they went.

Throughout my first re-unions with my friends and my parents' friends, the question uppermost in my mind was how much they had known about what had happened to the Jews during the war. Just asking the question was not that far removed from asking 'and did you approve of what was being done to them, and if not, how could you have stood by and done nothing?'

However, I felt unable to bring myself to raise this matter so early on in our reunion.

The following day I had some time to take in the scene in the centre of Vienna. One of the most typical sights was the jeeps containing four soldiers, one from each of the occupying powers, cruising around the city, presumably with the purpose of keeping an eye open for any misdemeanours perpetrated by members of their respective armed forces. There was no evidence of any camaraderie between them, and perhaps that was a microcosm of the situation between the occupying powers, which, together with the underlying atmosphere of black market crime, was in later years so well portrayed in the film *The Third Man* based on Graham Greene's novel of that name.

That evening I had arranged to meet Trudl Hobiger at a restaurant in the Prater, the famous Viennese amusement park by the Danube. She came along with her husband, and I was not prepared for how much she had changed in the intervening ten years. Although only a couple of years older than me, she was a mature woman. She had the same problem with me, but in reverse because she was expecting someone looking more my age, and it was only because we were both obviously searching for someone in the crowded restaurant that we managed to make contact.

Now married, Trudl told me she had lived in Czechoslovakia during the latter part of the war, where her father had been a bank manager. They managed to escape back to Austria before the Russians came in, and settled in Hallein, a small town in the American Occupation Zone near Salzburg, where Herr Hobiger bought a lorry and started a small transport business. After her marriage Trudl had moved back to her husband's home in Vienna. Although I knew Trudl had been in the BDM, the 'Association of German Girls', the female equivalent of the Hitler Youth, I didn't find out any more about what she did during the war.

The next day Herbert together with his wife Margret, and Walter with his girl friend Friedl and I all went on an outing to a 'Heurigen' (this year's wine) bar in Grinzing, a district of Vienna famous for this kind of establishment. It was a happy evening with a lot of laughter, risqué jokes provided by Walter and Herbert, and quite a lot of new wine. On the way home in the tram I disgraced myself by being violently sick, but was saved from fouling the other passengers by Walter's presence of mind in yanking me on to the tram's rear platform and supporting me whilst vomiting over the side. It was another occasion where I embarrassed myself by my apparent immaturity, being sick after a few glasses of wine, with my friends all remaining relatively sober and having to look after me.

The following week Walter, Herbert and I took the train to Salzburg. I had already planned ahead for me to stay at the White Horse inn at St. Wolfgang near Salzburg, whilst Herbert and Walter were going to share a room in a boarding house nearby. We also decided to use the opportunity to visit both Herbert's parents en route, with me going on my own to see the Hobigers, since neither Walter nor Herbert knew them.

The journey from Vienna entailed crossing from the Russian into the American Zone at the Bridge over the River Enns. On the Russian side we had our papers checked by a very Mongolian- looking Russian, and on the American side by a very black American, a situation which must have been particularly discomfiting to those Austrians still harbouring any traces of belief in the dominance of the Aryan race, but gave my friends some cause for amusement.

From Salzburg we took the slow train to where Herbert's parents lived. It was a sort of a camp with wooden chalet style buildings set amongst trees, so the situation was semi-rural. The interior furnishings were rudimentary, but Frau Krisch had made a sort of a home for herself and her husband. Unlike Walter's father, who had remained in his post at the Moedling Swimming Pool, Herbert's father had been in the army, engaged in rail communications in Yugoslavia when he was taken prisoner. He had only been released from the Yugoslav prison camp a few months before, and looked frail with his hair now turned completely white. He was pleased to see me, but I wasn't able to learn much about what had happened to him in the war. The mere fact that he had remained a prisoner for three years after the end of it was enough to explain his frailty. Although Frau Krisch was positive and light hearted, as always, one could see that she, too, had suffered in the intervening years. It was a sad interlude, and I suspected that Herbert's father was not long for this world. In the event, he died two years later.

My next port of call was Hallein, to visit Herr and Frau Hobiger. They lived out in the countryside in a little house along the main road about a mile's walk from the nearest railway station. Frau Hobiger hadn't changed a lot, although she had lost some weight. Herr Hobiger, who had always been lightly built, was almost gaunt. We talked around the kitchen table, mainly about my parents and Fred. It was only after Frau Hobiger brought lunch to the table and he said grace that I realised that he was a changed man. He had never been religious, and now gradually it all came out. Whatever had happened in Czechoslovakia had convinced him that the Russian invasion was God's punishment of the Germans for not abiding by what it said in the Bible. He then told me that if you read the scriptures thoroughly, you would see that it was all prophesied. The only thing left for them was to abide by God's word, and repent their sins.

While he was telling me all this, I several times caught Frau Hobiger's eye. I was beginning to feel like a conspirator, since I realised that she went along with all this only because she had always done what he wanted, and it was too late to change now. Another sad farewell – but at least their little business was enough to keep them going.

Throughout my visit to Austria, the question of what and how much my friends and their parents had known about the Holocaust during the war was uppermost in my mind. I finally steeled myself to thread the question into my discussions about the war with Herbert and Walter. Both said categorically they had known nothing about the gas chambers until the war was over. Of course they had known about concentration camps, but not what went on inside, nor that some were just transit camps to the gas chambers at Auschwitz. And of course they knew that those Jews that hadn't been able to leave the country were gradually being deported to Poland after 1940.

Both Herbert and Walter were a year younger than me, and weren't called up into the Wehrmacht until 1944. Before that their only contact with the war had been the presence of slave labourers in camps near Moedling, who had to work in the local underground factory making aircraft parts. Walter's girl friend Friedl, who later became his wife, worked as a secretary for a company employing this kind of labour, and told me they were treated well.

My friends also had to pay a price for what had happened. After the Russians came into Austria, rape became an everyday occurrence, and was still going on, though on a much reduced scale, at the time of my visit. Herbert and Walter had lost three years of their education, and Herbert now had epilepsy as a result of his treatment as a prisoner of war with the French. Nobody in their part of Austria was getting a square meal in the immediate post-war years, except those who were ingratiating themselves with the occupation army, as did many of those known to have been Nazi Party members.

So Herbert and Walter just wanted to forget all that and get on with their lives.

When it came to their parents or my parents' friends, I felt unable to even broach the subject of the holocaust at all since, by implication, I would have been questioning them with a view to assessing the extent of their compliance. They were, after all, friends, people my parents and I had known and liked, and I therefore accepted that whatever they did would have been very similar to what my parents would have done in their situation.

In subsequent years this acceptance of mine was challenged countless times by those who claimed to know better, and maintained that the bulk of the German and Austrian people must have known what was going on, and did nothing about it.

What they knew

The years following my first return visit to Moedling after the war were taken up with my engineering career and my marriage and family. There was, however, always a nagging feeling of unfinished business which surfaced whenever the war or the holocaust came to my mind. It was simply the question 'how was it possible for a civilised nation to engage in the unbelievable acts of brutality involved in the holocaust?' And how many actually knew what was being done in their name? And why did those that knew go along with it? And supposing I had stayed on and been trapped into my father's situation of being enrolled on 'the other side', as he had been at the beginning of the previous war, would I ever have condoned any of it?

Many years after my first return, and after renewing my contacts with the people I had known there in my childhood, I came across a detailed account of what happened to the Jews in Moedling from the time I left it until after the war. It was a book entitled *Ausgeloescht* (Extinguished)[1] – about the life of the Jews in Moedling, compiled by a group of local residents. The title says it all. In the course of the years 1938-39 the number of Jews registered as such by the Jewish Cultural Community of Moedling dwindled from just over a thousand to thirty five. Most of those that had disappeared initially moved to Vienna prior to emigration to whichever country would have them, provided they were in a position to pay the emigration tax imposed by the Nazis, plus travel and resettling expenses for those countries that were willing to take them. These conditions, of course, immediately excluded those with only modest means at their disposal. Of those left in Vienna, the bulk were eventually deported to the East, supposedly to engage in war work for the Third Reich. Of those that didn't go directly to the gas chambers, most eventually perished in the concentration camps due to starvation and disease.

Some initial acts of persecution had already taken place prior to my leaving Moedling for the first time. The only incident described in 'Ausgeloescht' which I had witnessed myself was when the proprietor of the sports shop where Herbert had bought his birthday javelin not many months before was forced to write 'Jew' in large letters on his shop window, with a Brownshirt supervising and a few shoppers stopping to watch. I was secretly ashamed of this, and so, I think, was Herbert, who just commented that this shopkeeper's prices had always been extortionate.

The book also mentioned numerous other events which happened after I had left Moedling, like the elderly Jewish woman shopkeeper who was made to sit in her shop window to be spat at by the children of the more rabid passing Nazis. Subsequently, any shoppers entering Jewish shops had to pass a Brownshirt at the entrance whose job it was to draw prospective customers' attention to the fact that they were entering a Jewish shop, and also make a mental note of those who went in regardless. Needless to say, most of the Jewish businesses disappeared rapidly, or just changed hands into Aryan ownership at knock down prices.

The situation of the Jews in Moedling, as well as throughout Austria and Germany, had deteriorated drastically after 8th November 1938 and what came to be known as the 'Kristallnacht' (Crystal night) referring to the breaking of glass associated with attacks on Synagogues and Jewish shops, supposedly in retaliation for the assassination of a German diplomat at their Embassy in Paris by a German Jewish youth who had learnt that his parents had been deported to Poland. Ironically, the diplomat involved was later found to have been anti-Nazi with pro-Jewish leanings.

Two incidents recounted in his book *Wien stark bewoelkt* ('Vienna strongly overcast)[2], by fellow Moedlinger Peter Weiser, a music critic who eventually became a member of the first Austrian post-war government under Chancellor Kreisky, illustrate the worsening situation. In the first one, Weiser, who was partly Jewish himself, is walking with an older Jewish boy, the brother of a friend who had had to leave the Grammar school in Moedling because these schools were now prohibited for Jews. They were walking toward two men previously known to him as acquaintances of his parents, both dressed in Brownshirt uniforms. One of them stopped and shouted at his friend 'and what do you Jewish brat think you're doing wearing leather shorts, when you know the Fuehrer has forbidden Jews to walk around with bare knees'. His friend, stunned by the unexpected encounter, stood still and just looked his interrogator in the eye, whereupon he had his face slapped. Drawing himself up to stand to attention, and, presumably in order to defuse the situation, he identified himself as 'Reserve

LIeutenant Hugerth', in order to indicate that he was a volunteer recruit for the army. This was taken as cheek by the man, who got out his rubber truncheon and hit his friend over the head with it, before rejoining his fellow Brownshirt.

In another incident in the summer of 1939, Weiser, a good swimmer, had been selected by the Moedling Club to compete for Vienna against Berlin. There had been some pressure from the Vienna club manager to let the Berliners win, so when Weiser decided to ignore this and won his race, the Vienna manager was furious, and became more so when he found out that Weiser was not in the Hitler Youth. 'Next thing you're going to tell me he's a Jew', he shouted. 'Just pull down your trunks so we can see if you're circumcised'. Weiser was dumbfounded – pull down his trunks in public, with girls present as well? In desperation, he jumped back into the pool. When the manager realised that Weiser's fellow club members were not going to obey his instructions and pull down Weiser's trunks, he backed down.

During a skiing holiday the following year, Weiser's mother met a high ranking SS Officer by the name of Daluege (later hanged by the Czech government for war crimes committed during his position as governor of Bohemia and Moravia). In the course of their meetings, he talked about the likely fate of the Jews now that Madagascar was no longer an option for them. Secretly distraught, she asked him what they would do with half-Jews. They, she was informed, would be treated like the 'Gammas' in Huxley's *Brave New World* after the war. In the meantime, he said, we will leave them in peace, as long as they are doing useful work. And what would happen to the 'quarter' Jews (bearing in mind her sons would be classified as 'three-eights', she asked. 'They will be treated like Huxley's Beta-Plus or Beta-Minus, depending on accomplishments such as knowledge of foreign languages, for instance.

After returning from her holiday, she managed to get hold of Huxley's book and ascertained that 'gammas' in the novel were conditioned to do the lowest and most demeaning tasks in society – basically they were used as slave labour. As a result of his mother's new-found knowledge, Weiser's lessons in French and English were stepped up.

The question of 'What they knew', has been exhaustively examined in a number of publications. Ian Kershaw, in his *Hitler, the Germans and the Final Solution*[3] states that the very secrecy of *the Final Solution* demonstrates more clearly than anything else the fact that the Nazi leadership knew well that it would never get the backing of the bulk of the German people for this..

The statistical analysis conducted by the authors of *What we knew: Terror, Mass Murder and Everyday Life in Nazi* Germany[4] relied principally on interviews with individual Germans. A significant number of those they interviewed were Jews, which in itself does raise the question as to whether they would have been an impartial source of evidence on this matter. The book's credibility is in addition diminished by the authors' conclusion that intimidation and terror played no great part in enforcing loyalty to the Nazis. This has been flatly contradicted by the records of resistance activities discussed in the chapter 'The un-sung Germans' below, in addition to what a number of writers whose credentials are acknowledged have to say about it. In his last book, *Alone in Berlin*[5], Hans Fallada (best known for his post-world war I book *Little Man what now?*) describes a production line in a factory known to be investigated for someone dropping anti- Nazi propaganda post cards. He writes: '*They all sense the threat hanging over them. Because there is not one among the eighty men who has not in some way opposed the present government, at least by a word or two! Each one is threatened. Each life is at risk. They are all terrified...*'

A piece of evidence quoted by the 'they must have known' lobby relates to BBC broadcasts to Europe mentioning gas chamber executions as early as 1942. These, however, were made in Czech and Croat, presumably because it was thought that the East Europeans were more likely to be able to do something about this. Even if these reports had seeped into Germany, they would have been treated as the British version of Goebbels propaganda, i.e. with incredulity, as indeed it was by a member of the British Joint Intelligence Committee up to as late as August 1943. By the time the first credible reports about Auschwitz were broadcast by the BBC in German in June 1944[6], the few Germans who had the temerity to listen to them knew what was in store for them had they been found out.

In his memoir *Not Me*[7], historian and journalist Joachim Fest, onetime publisher of the renowned *Frankfurter Allgemeine Zeitung,* writes about his upbringing in a Catholic family in Berlin. His father, a staunch social democrat, was bitterly opposed to the Nazi regime from the start, and brought his children up accordingly. He was sacked from his headmastership of a local grammar school within months of Hitler coming to power, and had to bring up his family of five during the rest of the Nazi regime on a meagre pension. But he never relented, in spite of having been told that he might resume his career if he agreed to join the party. Throughout the war he listened to BBC broadcasts regularly, knowing full well the risks of being sent to a Concentration Camp if found out during the early stages of the war, or summary trial and execution towards the end.

It could be said he was a good witness for the defence of the great majority of Germans who knew nothing about extermination camps, since he was highly enough motivated to uncover any 'dirt' about the Hitler regime to accept the risks involved. He was lucky not to be caught in the act, and actually heard about a British parliamentary debate over Christmas of 1942 on reports of the gassing of Jews in Auschwitz. He decided that this was just British propaganda emulating Goebbels's, a view shared, as mentioned above, by a senior member of the British Secret Service at the time. Then, in 1943, he heard about the atrocities committed by the SS in Russia from soldiers on leave, and eventually had to accept that they were true. Although he had a lively dialogue with his sons, he never told them about this, in case they were ever detained for questioning. Since they all remained staunchly anti-Nazi, there was a real danger of that, particularly after they were sent to a Catholic boarding school in Freiburg because Joachim had been reported telling anti-Hitler jokes in his Berlin school. Nor had they joined the Hitler Youth, a fact which entailed a further risk. Although they eventually heard about the atrocities in Russia from their Father's friends, they never knew about the extermination camps.

In her book *The German Trauma*[8], Gitta Sereny quotes Kurt Legge, the State Solicitor General leading the German Nazi crime investigations in the 1960s and 70s telling her that the principal perpetrators of the war crimes in Russia were members of the SS Einsatzkommando 1005. This was the most secret of all the 'Special Commands' active in Eastern Europe and the Balkans, who knew they would have been shot immediately had they talked about what they had seen or done.

In her definitive and exhaustive biography of *Albert Speer*[9], Hitler's architect and later Minister for War Production, Gitta Sereny devotes a large part to finding evidence of his involvement in 'the final solution', which he claimed to have known nothing about. She finally got no further than believing, in spite of contradictory evidence, that he must have known. But after her long odyssey in getting this far, she also agrees that most Germans did not know.

In Treblinka, according to the latest estimates *(2010, see Wikipedia Treblinka Extermination Camp)*[10] just 35 SS and 120 Ukraneans accounted for between 700,000 and 900,000 victims in the course of its one year existence. If that proportion were applied to the total exterminations now estimated at 6 million, it would mean that only around 1000 personnel would have been required to carry these out.

One of the accounts which indicates that there was no widespread knowledge of what was going on in Poland in 1942 concerned one Goeran von Otter, a Swedish diplomat. On an overcrowded train coming back to Berlin from Warsaw he got into conversation with another passenger in the corridor, who happened to be Kurt Gerstein, an SS Officer. When Gerstein learnt about the identity of his new acquaintance he told him that he had witnessed a trainload of Jews being gassed, and implored him to inform the Swedish government what was going on.

This act in itself would contradict the idea that the gas chambers were known about in Germany at that time. Von Otter duly reported what he had learnt to the Swedish Foreign Office.

It remained a matter of deep regret to him for the rest of his life that he did not pursue the matter further, particularly when he discovered after the war that the Swedish government had decided to keep this information under wraps. Whether or not this was done out of fear of upsetting the Germans, who were a significant customer for Swedish steel, we shall never know.

According to a an account of the meeting in the Berlin Resistance records Kurt Gerstein had been a supporter of the Protestant Youth movement and first surfaced in the Gestapo files as resisting its incorporation into the Hitler Youth. He volunteered for the Waffen SS in 1941 with the idea of learning more about the persecution of the Jews. In view of his engineering background coupled with subsequent medical studies he was engaged in the development of disinfection equipment for the Wehrmacht, prisoner of war and concentration camps. He had been to Belzec and Treblinka with a consignment of Zyklon B just prior to his meeting with von Otter. For the remainder of his life right up to end of the war he tried to inform representatives of the Vatican, German Bishops, the Dutch resistance and the Swiss embassy what he had seen at Auschwitz and Triblenka, but not one of them believed him.

Another account from the book *Composers of the Nazi Era: Eight Portraits*[11] by Michael H Kater records how the composer Richard Strauss was in ignorance concerning the final destination of the Jews in Theresienstadt as late as 1944. Strauss had driven there to visit his daughter-in-law's Jewish grandmother. When he reported to the SS gatepost, he quickly learnt it was not a holiday camp open to all-comers. Even after he had identified himself to the SS guards, they remained unmoved and sent him packing. Like the rest of the Germans and Austrians, he had been under the impression Theresienstadt was still only a ghetto, whereas at that time it had already started deporting some of its residents to Auschwitz. It had originally been a ghetto established around some barracks dating back to the first world war, and only after 1942 also became a transit station for Jews destined for Auschwitz. Indeed, it was publicised by the Viennese city authorities as a desirable retirement home for Viennese Jews as late as 1944, at a price, of course. It had also been used by Goebbels as a location for a propaganda film with the title *The Fuehrer gives the Jews a town*, which was to demonstrate to the world how well the Jews were really being treated by the Nazis – an enterprise he would have been unlikely to undertake if extermination of the Jews was common knowledge in Germany and Austria.

After some agitation by the Danish Government about the treatment of Danish Jews in Theresienstadt, the Nazis had agreed to permit inspections by the International Red Cross in June 1944, followed by a second one in April 1945. The Germans finally handed the running of the camp over to the Red Cross five days before the liberation of the camp by the Russians. Even then, the Red Cross had remained unaware that it had been used as a transit camp to Auschwitz. Another piece of evidence relating to how little they knew concerns Ilse Weber, one of the Jewish inmates at Theresienstadt. Working as a nurse in the makeshift children's hospital there, she wrote poetry and songs to entertain the children, including her younger son, the older one, Hanus, having been sent to England in one of the Kindertransports before his parents were taken to Theresienstadt. An account of Ilse Weber's life there, based on her correspondence, is documented by Ulrike Migdal in *Ilse Weber – Wenn wohl das Leid ein Ende hat*, (Ilse Weber – When will the suffering end)[12.]

Ilse and her husband Willi were not permitted to cohabit in Theresienstadt, but saw each other regularly. In September 1944 the Germans told the Ghetto management to select 5000 able-bodied men below the age of fifty for 'earthworkings' in Germany, on the understanding that their families would be allowed to continue living in Theresienstadt, and they would be able to remain in contact by correspondence. Willi, who had heard rumours about the final destination of previous transports, believed this one to be a genuine proposal and volunteered, but gave Ilse strict instructions not to follow him on any subsequent transports.

But Willi was actually sent to Auschwitz, and immediately realised what was happening there. Only the fittest members of his transport were selected for work, with the rest dispatched to the gas chambers. The camp management then asked for men with experience in metalworking for another camp at Weiglitz, and again Willi volunteered. This saved his life, because four months later Weigliz was liberated by the Russian Army. Ilse, however, had in the meantime volunteered to go on the next transport to follow him with their younger son, not knowing what awaited them at the end, but hoping that at least they would be together again as a family.

When Ilse's older son Hanus was finally re-united with his father in Prague after the end of the war, his father told him that he was still trying to trace his mother and brother. In time, they had to accept that they had died in the gas chambers.

This is described in Hanus Weber's book: *Ilse–a love story without a happy ending,.* first published by Ilse's Legacy in English via Foefattares Bockmaskin, Stockholm in 2009, but no longer in print. It predates Ulrike Migdal's book, and recounts the family's history from his own perspective. The author kindly sent me a copy after learning of my interest. One of the most poignant stories documented in both books relates to what Hanus heard from an old friend of his father's some years after his father had died. This man, after getting Hanus's agreement to keep his name secret, told him he had been working at Auschwitz on the gas chamber corpse removal squad. One day, after arrival of another trainload from Theresienstadt, he had recognised Ilse, who was looking after a group of children including her son Tommy, Hanus's brother. He was able to have a brief conversation with her, because the guards were some distance away. 'Is it true we are going to get a shower here?' she asked him. He decided to tell her the truth, and advised her to get the children singing as they went into the chamber and to keep them singing as long as possible. It would make for an easier death. 'I couldn't bring myself to tell your father this when we met again after the war', he told Hanus.

A further unexpected witness to how little they knew surfaces in the book *Until the final hour*[13] by Traudl Junge, who was Hitler's secretary from the end of 1942 until his suicide in April 1945. She portrays Hitler as a sociable person who liked to mix with his staff, generally taking his meals with them, and conversing with them on all sorts of topics. He was even open to argument if one of his regular retinue went as far as to question something he had said. There was one incident, however, which did arouse his ire. It occurred during a mealtime gathering early in 1943 when the wife of Baldur von Schirach, the Gauleiter of Vienna, was present. She had turned to Hitler and said, 'My Fuehrer, I saw a train full of deported Jews in Amsterdam the other day. Those poor people – they looked terrible. I'm sure they are very badly treated. Do you know about it? Do you allow it?' This question caused a painful silence. Soon afterwards, Hitler rose to his feet, said goodnight and withdrew. Next day Frau von Schirach went back to Vienna, having been informed that she 'had failed to carry out her duty of entertaining the Fuehrer'. She evidently had no idea of the final destination of the subjects of her concern, and Hitler would have been the last person to reveal what was a top secret to this tiresome woman.

Baldur von Schirach remained in office until the end of the war, although he had incurred Hitler's displeasure because of his criticism of the treatment of the Jews. At the Nuremberg trials he claimed that he had not known that the camps in Poland he had arranged for Viennese Jews to be deported to were death camps.

The already mentioned Christabel Bielenberg, the British wife of a German aristocrat, recounts in her book *The Road ahead*[14] of listening to the radio with other locals from the small Bavarian village where she lived with her family when the war ended. It happened to be about what the Allies had discovered about the gas chambers. After years of Nazi propaganda, she and the other listeners were used to being fed with lies on the radio. Their first reaction was incredulity.

Another piece of evidence that most Germans knew nothing about the Holocaust was that those that did, within the Nazi inner circle, did their utmost to keep it secret because they knew that if it became common knowledge, they would have had to face fierce opposition from within. Yet every other act of aggression and brutality against the Jews and the Bolshevics was trumpeted and justified by Goebbel's propaganda machine. In Richard Breitman's book *The Architect of Genocide – Himmler and the*

Final Solution[15] the author quotes from an interrogation of Auschwitz Commandant Rudolf Hoess, who said that when Himmler first told him that Auschwitz was to be used as an extermination centre in July 1941, he also instructed him to treat this order as absolutely secret, even from his superiors. Not surprisingly, when the International Red Cross inspection team were sent to report on conditions there in September 1944 they were fooled into believing they were looking at communal shower facilities when these were in fact the gas chambers.

The term 'the final solution' was first used officially at the Wannsee Conference in Berlin in February of 1942. The Conference was convened by Himmler to establish a plan for moving all European Jews into the German- occupied regions of Poland, Lithuania and Russia, initially to provide a source of slave labour for the war effort under conditions which would ensure a natural decline in the numbers held there, before disposing of the remainder after the war. But the execution of Jews in Poland had already been unofficially sanctioned by Gauleiters in Poland when faced with trainloads of Jews from Germany arriving at Lodz destined for the local ghetto which was already hugely overcrowded. They took the decision to have trainloads of them shot in a remote siding to deal with the logistical problem that was landed on them. This then developed into the more convenient method of gassing the new arrivals in special lorries, and eventually into installing gas chambers in the vicinity of slave labour camps such as Auschwitz.

It is even debatable to what extent, with the exception of Himmler and his associates, Hitler's entourage knew what was going on in Poland. The historian Mark Mazower's book *Hitler's Empire:Nazi rule in occupied Europe*[16] throws some light on this. But even Goering claimed at the Nuremberg trials that he hadn't known what the final solution was going to be, although he had signed the order to initiate one. Hitler himself never went public about it – he was sane enough to know that had it ever leaked out, his days as Fuehrer would have been in jeopardy.

The 'Evacuation', a code term used for 'Extermination' of the Jewish race, was regarded by Himmler as a top secret, and as 'an unwritten and never to be written page of glory in our history', as he was (unwittingly) recorded saying in the course of his address to his SS Gruppenfuehrer at Posen in October 1943. This was not the sort of statement he would have made had he believed that the German people either knew about it already, or were ever likely to do so in the future.

Henry Metelmann, a Wehrmacht soldier, described his experiences on the Russian front in his book *Through Hell for Hitler*[17]. He knew nothing about what went on in Poland or even behind the front lines, but illustrates how brutalization became more marked when survival was at stake. So, for example, during the early advance of the Wehrmacht, as the German soldiers occupied villages, they would commandeer the peasants' cottages to the extent of sharing the available shelter and warmth, letting the occupants, usually women, children and the elderly, sleep in their large bed in one corner whilst bedding down on the remaining floor space, and sometimes even sharing their army rations with them, since many of the peasants were already on a starvation diet. Later, during the retreat from Russia, however, they would simply eject the occupants, leaving them to cope with the sub-zero temperatures as best they could. Then, on leaving the villages, they had been instructed to burn down whatever they had time for (another Nazi directive: you must show no mercy to these sub-humans).

Brutalization eventually affected the treatment of their own comrades. Metelmann recounts how, at one stage during the retreat, one of the more fanatical Nazi officers ordered a counter attack in accordance with Hitler's orders to hold their ground to the last man. The soldiers under his command, knowing full well that they would all perish if they obeyed him, simply shot him. During the final stages of the retreat there were no means available to take care of the wounded. When one of his comrades was badly injured, rather than leaving him to the tender mercies of the climate and/or the partisans, Metelmann shot him.

In an ironic prelude to the above, Metelmann recounts a religious service held during the heady days of the advance into Russia, with the army chaplain leading prayers to Almighty God to preserve the Fuehrer and the Fatherland. At the end of the service, he invited any soldiers who had problems to come and discuss them with him. Metelmann took him at his word, and when his turn came, he asked him how it was possible for the soldiers to live by the Bible when it commanded them not to kill. The chaplain looked him in the eye, murmured 'Bless you, my boy' and moved on to the next supplicant, no doubt hoping for subsequent questions to be easier to deal with.

Another account of the Russian campaign in the Memoirs of Klaus von Bismarck, a member of the German aristocracy, shows the effect of his difference in upbringing from that of Metelman, who was from working class origins with a Social Democrat father. Von Bismarck's Prussian upbringing had inculcated a fanatical devotion to discipline, obedience and unquestioning sacrifice. In his memoirs *Aufbruch aus Pommern*[18] (Departure from Pomerania) he recounts that his religious upbringing also led him to question what was going on, though never the whole morality of the war. On one occasion, after being told of Hitler's 'Commissar Order' to execute captured Communist commissars, he got the agreement of his fellow officers to inform their commanding officer that they could not obey such an order, since it went against everything they believed in. The commanding officer decided to turn a blind eye to this revolt in the ranks, presumably because the only alternative would have been to report them for insubordination, which would have resulted in their wholesale arrest and execution. Perhaps he was also a pragmatist to the extent of 'wait and see what happens when the occasion actually arises'. In the event, the Commissar Order was rescinded within a year, after it became evident that the Bolsheviks had got wind of it, and were retaliating by not bothering to take prisoners but shooting any wounded or surrendering Germans on the spot.

In spite of this incident, Klaus von Bismarck continued fighting in the Wehrmacht until the end of the war. He gained numerous medals and distinctions, and, after being sent home for convalescence from an injury towards the end of the war, was taken prisoner by the British. He had heard about atrocities committed by SS 'Einsatz' units, but continued to believe for some years after the end of the war that the Wehrmacht was not involved in these. It was not until 1986, in the course of an official visit to Minsk, that he was taken to visit a memorial in the remains of the village of Chatwyn in the forest nearby. During the war the villagers commemorated by the memorial, mostly women, children and the elderly, had been herded into a house decked with petrol-soaked straw which was then set alight. Any of those who had tried to escape had been shot. This action was carried out by a special 'Security' division of the Wehrmacht.

This incident on its own would have been more than enough to shake Bismarck's faith in the Wehrmacht, but a total of 186 similar incidents were listed. He was incredulous and proceeded to track down surviving Wehrmacht officers of the Security Division responsible in order to find out the truth. To his dismay the only three he found not only corroborated these incidents but took the view that the Security Division had been fully justified in carrying out these actions, since every man, woman and child of these 'sub-human mobs' was working with the partisans in cowardly blowing up German supply columns at night. Under the circumstances, and bearing in mind that they were only carrying out Hitler's instructions, they could have done no less.

Bismarck was devastated. The only explanation he could find was that these officers were still referring to all Bolsheviks as 'sub-human', so they evidently belonged to the remains of those that had been successfully brainwashed by National Socialist propaganda in their formative years.

We shall never know how many Germans had any knowledge of what went on in the extermination camps, or even the concentration camps during the war. Was it hundreds, thousands, tens of thousands or millions? Nor will we ever know how many of those that knew, approved or kept quiet in order to survive. What is not disputable, however, is that the Nazi regime did its utmost to keep the holocaust a secret, which means that they feared that had it become public knowledge it would have meant the end of their rule.

What we knew

British Intelligence knew about the plans for the final solution as early as June 1941 from the 'Ultra' Project which had enabled them to decipher the German 'Enigma' code used in their radio communications. As already mentioned, however, some members of the British Joint Intelligence committee did not really believe it until more than two years later. This might have been one of the reasons for the failure to take remedial action by destroying the railway lines into Auschwitz. Another reason given was that British Intelligence believed that this would have given a signal to the Nazi intelligence that they had cracked the Enigma code, and thus destroyed any further access to Nazi plans in the future. The latter explanation would imply that the military strategists thought they would, in the end, thereby save more Allied lives by bringing the war to an end more quickly.

So, apart from the Allied intelligence services, neither the British public nor the rest of the world apart from some of the top Nazis knew what might have been happening in terms of the gassing of Jews and other undesirables in Poland during the latter stages of the war. What did become common knowledge in the public domain in Britain during those years, however, was the gradual change in the policy of 'strategic' bombing of German industrial sites to 'carpet' bombing, which did no longer discriminate between military and civilian targets. This change in strategy, at the behest of 'Bomber' Harris but with the approval of Churchill and the wartime coalition cabinet, was motivated by the idea that the resulting pressure from the civilian workforce in Germany would result in the unconditional surrender demanded by the Allies. In the event, this move turned out to have the opposite effect, in that it resulted in stiffening resistance because of what the Germans regarded, rightly, as terror aimed at their civilian population.

Although no figures for likely civilian casualties were broadcast, the general view in Britain was, 'well, they started it, didn't they'. There were some voices raised in protest at the time, notably those of Vera Brittain (see *Vera Brittain- A Life*[19]), Lord

Salisbury, George Bell (the Bishop of Chichester), and a few others. They did not gain much support in Britain. In America, supposedly the largest Christian Nation on Earth, these lone voices did make the headlines, but only in order to castigate the originators as 'Nazis' and traitors to the Allied war effort.

Since the indiscriminate area bombing inevitably resulted in a massive civilian death toll, it was seen by the German population as a crime against humanity, thus. enabling Goebbels to revive the flagging support for a final stand against the Allied armies. In retrospect, therefore, the argument that it helped to shorten the war is open to debate..

Post-war studies have shown that the total number of civilians killed in air raids on Germany were between 300,000 and 600,000. The huge variance in these figures alone indicates that they were no longer able to keep count towards the end of the war. They do show, however, that we managed to kill between ten and twenty German civilians for every British civilian killed by them.

Compared with the total number of people murdered by the Nazi regime these figured may appear insignificant. It has to be borne in mind, though, that some Germans might have argued that, in retrospect, given the choice between being burned or gassed to death, they would have opted for the latter. Nevertheless, it was not until many years after the end of the war that German writers went as far as suggesting that the bombing was as much a crime against humanity as the gassing of the Jews. Not many British writers followed suit, although Christabel Bielenberg, who lived in Berlin with her family throughout most of the bombing, did make some critical comments in her book *The past is myself*[20].

The unsung Germans

After sixty years of relative silence on the issue, the time is ripe for a tribute to those Germans who paid the price for remaining civilised when those around them preferred to continue looking after their own immediate concerns. How many thousands, or perhaps even millions, of these there were we shall never know. Their memory lies buried, where not in the concentration camps, under the shame of the survivors. But let's mention just a few whose names never made their way into the history books.

Who better to help us in this than Gitta Sereny, the English educated Austro Hungarian Francophile author of *The German Trauma*[8] (already mentioned above), who set herself the task of understanding the people engaged in the holocaust. Like me, she had become an incipient Nazi in her formative years, and like me had been cured with a dose of English environment, in her case a boarding school in Kent.

Her own experiences in the early stages of the descent into the abyss involved just a few of the 'unsung'. There were the two German officers who had helped her when, as a young woman working at a home for abandoned refugee children in occupied France, she was engaged in obtaining medical supplies and food for the children. Both of the Germans made no secret of the fact that they disliked the Hitler regime, and she later found out that they had paid the price. One was sent to the Russian front, the other to a concentration camp.

Not long after that, she made her escape across the Pyrenees helped by a French underground guide. Halfway across they were apprehended by two young German soldiers. She told them she was on her way to meet her British fiancee in Madrid, which was true, and that her guide would help her again when she returned in a week's time, which, needless to say, she had no intention of doing. The soldiers took all this at face value, and after sharing their bread and wine with them, let them go on, putting themselves at risk if their superior officers had ever found out.

Throughout the Nazi Regime, from its very beginnings to its end, there were countless Germans involved in resisting it. Accounts for Berlin alone have been compiled for the German Resistance Memorial gallery in Berlin, in the form of books for each of the twenty odd sectors of Berlin. They list resistors from distinct groups ranging from Socialists, Communists, Protestants, Catholics, and just those opposed to what was happening in terms of the persecution of the Jews. Each one of the books deals with hundreds who put their lives at risk, and many had to pay with them. Typical of the sort of resistors described is Eva-Maria Buch, who helped to translate contributions to the underground publication known as 'The Inner Front' into French in order to keep the French underground informed.. She was eventually arrested and guillotined in 1943 at the age of twenty two.

Laughable, if that term could be used under the tragic circumstances, is the figure of almost 5000 death sentences issued by the People's Court of Berlin between 1942 and 1944 on citizens found to have engaged in treasonous humour.

Considering that these accounts are for Berlin alone, we must now extrapolate them to all the major cities of Germany, which makes an assessment an insurmountable task. Only some of these resistors were Jews, and we should not forget that when we honour them all. Added to the German resistors are the Austrians put into concentration camps, estimated by the Austrian Historian Helmut Konrad in 2008 at over 100,000.

Amongst the better known martyrs of the German resistance were the students Hans and Sophie Scholl. They belonged to the 'White Rose' underground anti-Nazi society, and were arrested for distributing anti-Nazi leaflets at their University in Munich in February 1943. After a summary trial they were executed by guillotining. They were amongst the first of some 7000 victims of the infamous 'People's Courts'.

Sometimes whole families became victims of the Gestapo and the SS. One such family were the Schlotterbecks of Stuttgart. After the arrest and detention of their son Friedrich in 1933 for having been a member of the Communist Youth League, the family engaged in subversive anti-Nazi activities throughout the war. After his release in 1943, Friedrich re-joined the family and helped them in these activities, until they were betrayed to the Gestapo. Friedrich succeeded in escaping to Switzerland, but his parents, brother, sister and fiancee were all executed in concentration camps.

Of those Germans who opposed Nazi policies for religious reasons the earliest and best known was pastor Niemoeller, followed by Bernhard Lichtenberg, Dean of St.Hedwigs in Berlin, who both paid the price and died in concentration camps. Another ecclesiastic and theologian, Dietrich Bonhoeffer, became a target of the Gestapo soon after his inauguration for his relentless opposition to the Nazi regime from its beginning. Although Bonhoeffer was already forbidden to preach, his friend Dohnany managed to obtain a post for him in the Abwehr, the German Military Intelligence, on the basis that his international ecumenical contacts would provide useful information. Dohnany's aim was to use these contacts to try to establish negotiations for peace in a post-Hitler government, which he and fellow plotters in the Abwehr were hoping to establish after getting rid of Hitler. In the course of his travels to Norway, Sweden and Switzerland, Bonhoeffer met George Bell, the Bishop of Chichester in Sweden in 1942. As a result, Bell relayed information about the German resistance to Anthony Eden, together with the request for the British Government to make a public statement to the effect that it and its allies would make a distinction between the Nazi regime and the German people if and when the conspirators had succeeded in removing Hitler. The British government chose to ignore the request. Both Bonhoeffer and Dohnany were arrested early in 1943, and both were executed just weeks before the end of the war.

At the top of the chain of secret anti-Nazi plotters was Admiral Canaris, the head of the Abwehr. Although initially a Hitler supporter, he made the first of many moves to try to get rid of him in 1938. Thereafter he was instrumental in enabling the escape of some prominent Jews by hiring them as supposed secret agents and sending them out of Germany on fabricated intelligence missions. In 1943 he made contact with British agents in Paris, and asked them for information on likely terms for Germany if he succeeded in getting rid of Hitler. Churchill's reply was uncompromising: unconditional surrender. The SS finally arrested Canaris in 1944 and executed him just before the end of the war.

Of those who plotted the assassination of Hitler, Stauffenberg is the best known since he actually planted the bomb that nearly killed him. But there were many others involved who also paid with their lives. Robert Bernardis (who, incidentally, had connections with Moedling), was executed shortly after the assassination attempt in July 1944. Eventually even Rommel himself, although not directly involved, was given the choice of arrest or suicide. Since he chose the latter, we can safely assume that his involvement was sufficient for him to be treated as a fellow resistor.

Prior to Stauffenberg's attempt, there had been many other assassination attempts on Hitler, which all failed due to various accidents of history. The first one involved the Bavarian carpenter Georg Elser, who planted a bomb in the Munich beer cellar where Hitler was due to make an anniversary address shortly after the beginning of the war. Hitler, however, left the cellar some thirteen minutes before the bomb was due to go off. Had he still been there, he would very probably have been one of the eight fatal victims. Elser was caught crossing the border back to his home in Switzerland, and was put in a concentration camp for the rest of the war since Goebbels was intent on later proving that he had been in the pay of British Intelligence. He was shot by the SS on Goebbels' orders shortly before the end of the war.

These were just some of the better known victims, executed for having been caught in activities obviously hostile to the regime. But many were executed for minor offences, such as for example refusing to swear the oath of allegiance to Hitler. The oath was configured in such a way as making a refusal synonymous with not believing in a God. How many died because they refused to swear it, we shall never know, but amongst those in the public domain and on record were:

Franz Jaegerstaetter, an Austrian conscientious objector

Joseph Mayr-Nusser, an Austrian, after call-up to the Waffen-SS

Franz Reinisch, Austrian Padre, after call-up to the Wehrmacht

Joseph Ruf, German, 'Brother' of the 'Christ the King' religious sect.

Ernst Volkmann, Austrian, after call-up to the Wehrmacht

As for the many thousands of Germans and Austrians who were put into concentration camps for being union organisers, Socialists or Communists, they too should be acknowledged and mourned, quite apart from those who were put there just for giving up their seats to old or infirm Jews on trams and buses, or even committing the crime of having Jews as friends.

One of the better known examples of the latter is that of the German army Captain Wilm Hosenfeld who risked his life helping Jews in Poland, and in particular the Polish pianist Wladyslaw Szpilman. Although Szpilman drew attention to Hosenfeld's heroism immediately after the end of the war, it was not politically acceptable to praise Germans at the time, and Hosenfeld died virtually unknown in Russian captivity. It was only after publication of Szpilman's book *The Pianist* [23] that Rosenfeld became known, but even after that little has been said about him.

There are no figures available of how many of those that died in the concentration camps were ordinary Germans and Austrians who had made their opposition to the regime out of religious or political convictions public, or had been caught engaging in anti-Nazi activities, as opposed to just being Jews or Gypsies. Suffice to say they must be in the hundreds of thousands, and it is time we acknowledged them too.

The compilation of the information in this chapter has served the additional purpose of allowing me to settle a debt of gratitude to all those German family members together with friends, both German and Austrian, who had become my role models during my formative years. How could I do less than finally torpedo the British and indeed universal notion that they all belonged to an evil race, and worse, that their descendants should continue to feel ashamed for what their parents supposedly did or didn't do.

Part 3

Victims of history

The conclusions of Part II that most Germans knew little or nothing about the extermination camps in Poland and the executions being carried out by the SS Einsatz Commandos in Russia, left the question of how these atrocities ever came about unanswered. History shows that since the dawn of civilisation there have been many genocides, and they are still happening now. None, however, were of the intensity achieved by the Nazis within a mere four years, nor did the other perpetrators belong to a nation that had been one of the leading contributors to western religion, philosophy, science and the arts.

To offer some explanation, followed by some suggestions as to what, if anything, home sapiens can do to reduce the likelihood of further genocides or a nuclear catastrophe in the future, is the ambitious aim of what follows.

Evil

Hitler could safely be said to epitomize most people's notion of evil as the man virtually solely responsible for unleashing a war of untold brutality on an unsuspecting world, in addition to persecuting and exterminating Jews and other non-Aryans on a massive scale.

In spite of that he had a side to his nature which appealed to the mass of the German people and even members of their establishment. Indeed some members of the British and American Establishments also openly admired him before the war. He was polite to women and good with children. He was an animal lover and vegetarian largely because he disapproved of hunting and the slaughter of animals for food – a puzzling trait considering his eventual approval of the slaughter of his fellow humans. He was well known for being an admirer of Wagner's music with its embodiment of the heroic myths of the Germanic legends. He also took an interest in architecture, if only of the 'heroic' and 'triumphalist' kind, and remained faithful to his mistress Eva Braun until their end together.

In 'Mein Kampf' he writes of his politically formative years in Vienna as providing him with everything he needed to formulate his 'Weltanschauung' (World View), with no need to ever change it. This statement alone, considering the period covered was just from the age of sixteen until twenty- one, should have given rise to serious doubts about his intellectual maturity.

One of his principal formative experiences was when, during his early days in Vienna, he came face to face with orthodox Jews dressed in caftans, with greasy curly hair, who stank, and were, apparently, not to be seen in his native Linz. This experience alone was enough to initiate his implacable hatred of a race which, although its members were fellow citizens of the Austro-Hungarian Empire, he considered totally foreign to him. His dislike of other 'non-Germanic' fellow citizens included practically all those not of German origin, including Hungarians, Czechs, Serbs, Croats, Poles, and finally but especially Gypsies. How he came to extend his view of the Jewish race from encounters with a few down-at-heel orthodox Jews to include the Jewish writers, artists, scientists and intellectuals of international repute who at that time made up a sizeable portion of the Austrian elite can only be explained by a personality not able to face reality over simply acquired prejudice, which could best be described as deranged.

His hatred of the Jews was not, however, all of his own making. In 1909 he had come across a publication by Lanz von Liebenfels, an Austrian ex-Catholic novice and eccentric founder of the *Neutempler Orden* (Order of the New Templars). This was aimed at protecting the intrinsic superiority of the White Aryan Race by discouraging inter-racial breeding. Its publicity organ was the monthly 'Ostara' publication, of which Hitler became an early subscriber, no doubt attracted by its rabid anti-Semitic tone. This was during Hitler's early days in Vienna, when he was making a precarious living as a down-at-heel artist selling his sketches and titnted postcards of Viennese historical buildings, coupled with occasional stints as a housepainter. He is on record as having visited von Liebenfels to obtain a back copy of one of his publications, and having his return fare paid for him.

Lanz von Liebenfels had purchased the remains of Werfenstein Castle on the Danube as a conference centre for his followers, and displayed the Swastika Flag there on these occasions, some thirty years before it became commonplace in Austria after the Anschluss. The principal theme of Lanz's mystical 'Theosophy' was the demonstrable defilement of the Aryan race through interbreeding with the lower, 'ape man' races, largely due to Aryan women succumbing to their evil wily attractions. Not surprisingly, one of *Ostara's* main targets was women's liberation, whilst condoning the prostitution of non-Aryan women to Aryan men separated from their wives, perhaps deferring to the natural needs of the Knights Templars on their Crusades.

Although Lanz made a determined effort to get the support of the German, Austrian and even Russian aristocracy for his ideas, on the basis that they already practised selective in-breeding amongst their members, he failed to do so. He did, however, succeed in at least getting some better known people like Strindberg and Lenin interested, though in the latter's case mainly to find out what the opposition was up to. He also sent some of his publications to other likely supporters such as Lord Kitchener and Houston Chamberlain, the British racist polemicist.

Lanz disappeared from public view after the annexation of Austria, reputedly because Hitler intimated to him that their past association was not to be publicised. Liebenfels acquiesced, and died in obscure retirement without uttering a word, apart from confirming his meeting with Hitler to Wilfried Daim, the psychologist author of *Der Mann der Hitler die Ideen gab (The Man who gave Hitler the Ideas*[24]*)*, in the course of a meeting in 1951.

Another formative event in Hitler's early life was his discovery of *The Protocols of the Elders of Zion*, which had first surfaced in St.Petersburg in 1903, and had been promulgated throughout Europe. The Protocls purported to be a plan for a Jewish conspiracy to take over the world by subverting the social and financial institutions of the major nations, but had been discredited well before 1921 as an anti-Semitic forgery. Hitler dismissed the forgery evidence on the basis that the German Press would be forced to put this about since it was already dominated by Jews, and it remained a continuing theme throughout 'Mein Kampf', and indeed throughout the rest of his life.

The idea of the Jews being the principal promulgators of capitalism was then extended by Hitler with the notion that they were also the prime movers of communism, which moved the conspiracy theory well into the realms of phantasy. Nevertheless, Hitler's phantasy was not regarded as such by substantial sections of both the Catholic and the Protestant Churches.

One of Hitler's overriding emotions, apart from rage against his opponents, was his love of Wagner's music, inspired by his burning admiration of the heroic deeds of Nordic mythological knights such as Siegfried and Parsifal, which he was able to nurture by frequent visits to the Bayreuth Opera. On one of his visits he was introduced to Winifred Wagner, Wagner's English born daughter-in law, who was by then managing the Bayreuth Opera, and whose home in Bayreuth Hitler subsequently visited during the Bayreuth Opera seasons from 1923 to 1933. There was even some talk of a romantic attachment between the two, as portrayed in A.N.Wilson's *Winnie and Wolf*[25].

Another one of Hitler's English-born connections at Bayreuth was Houston Chamberlain, a British expatriate who had adopted German citizenship and was also connected to the Wagner family through his marriage to Wagner's step-daughter. Chamberlain was the author of *The Foundations of the Nineteenth Century*[26], a massive tome initially written by him in German in 1899, which became a widely distributed best-seller throughout Germany, and was later translated into English, selling up to a quarter of a million copies from its first publication right through to 1938. It purported to be a scientific study of races leading up to the notion that the survival of the Aryan race could only be ensured by eliminating the Jewish opposition, and even goes to some lengths to prove that Jesus' parents were not Jewish.

The English translation of 'The Foundations' found admirers in a wide spectrum of society, some very likely lured by Chamberlain's virulent opposition to Darwin and the Theory of Evolution, and some, such as George Bernard Shaw and other members of the Fabian Society, by his promotion of Eugenics as a means to improve the human race.

Chamberlain's work was described in the Nazi press as the gospel of National Socialism, and was adopted by Hitler's in-house philosopher Alfred Rosenberg as one of the mainstays of Nazi mythology after a meeting with the author together with Hitler at Winifred Wagner's house in 1923. Chamberlain later joined the Nazi Party, and his funeral in Bayreuth in 1927 was attended by Hitler together with some of his party bigwigs.

Htler's subsequent rise to power has been attributed to the uniqueness and power of his own personality and intellect, which goes along with the generally accepted idea that history consists of a sequence of events initiated by people who either inherit power or acquire it by the strength of their will. I prefer the view taken by some historians that history is a succession of unpredictable accidents which sweep some individuals on to the top of a wave, giving them the impression that this was as a result of their unique personality and intellect. King Canute was one of the few who had the wisdom to accept that even the power of a king to control the turn of events was limited, and rebuked his courtiers for believing he was able to control the tides of the sea.

The first accident of history in connection with Hitler's rise to power could well be ascribed to Hitler's father's decision to change his name from 'Schicklgruber' to Hitler. The original name, even in German, had a slightly comical sound, in addition to being derived from the a colloquial term for 'manure digger'. Just trying to imagine 'Heil Hitler' being replaced by 'Heil Schicklgruber' is enough to make people laugh, and would have proved a major stumbling block in any political career.

The second accident of history that set Hitler on his course was when, after a couple of years pursuing a lacklustre career as an artistic draughtsman in Munich, he found himself in a crowd listening to the proclamation that Germany had declared war on

Serbia. The photograph of him in the crowd says it all – in the words of Alan Bullock in his book *Hitler – a study in tyranny* [27], 'it is the face of a man who has come home at last'. Here was his chance to 'belong' to something larger than the movement of the eccentric Lanz von Liebenfels. He seized the opportunity to volunteer for the German Army, which required him, as a born Austrian, to request a special dispensation, which was granted. Now he not only belonged to Germany, he was also given the opportunity to vent his hatred of the Serbians in particular and all Slavs and non-Aryans in general, whose expatriate immigrants had been defiling the German culture of his native Austria.

The standard of Hitler's post-first world war public speeches at the Munich Beer Cellar about how Germany had been betrayed by its communist politicians to surrender to the Entente Cordiale were of a standard no higher than could be heard on Speakers' Corner in Hyde Park in London any weekend evening from Hitler's time to the present day. Here all and sundry are free to voice their anger against 'them', i.e. those who disagree with their views. It just so happened that at that time in Munich he had a sympathetic audience. His acquaintance with the right-wing General Ludendorff gave him an extra boost, leading to the 'Beer cellar coup', when Htler and his associates marched on the Munich town hall as the first step in what they expected to become a revolution. They had failed to anticipate armed opposition from the police and the army, and several of the participants in the march were killed or wounded. Hitler, unlike Goering, got away unscathed, but was subsequently tried and condemned to a term at Landsberg prison. He used his time there to write the first volume of *Mein Kampf*, consisting of some 300 pages.

One chapter of *Mein Kampf* shows that Hitler knew where his strength lay. It is where he refers to 'pig-headed intellectuals, who live apart from the practical world, and think that a writer must of necessity be superior to an orator in intelligence', an observation which he probably felt might also apply to him. He asserts his total disagreement with these intellectuals by stating that 'the masses of illiterate Russians were not fired to communist revolutionary enthusiasm by reading the theories of Karl Marx but by the promises of paradise made to the people by thousands of agitators in the service of an idea'. He obviously admired Bolshevik tactics, and later used them to good effect in his own cause, by appealing to 'the masses' in language and with promises they could understand.

Hitler wisely refrained from attacking religion in his book and throughout his subsequent career. He even maintained relations of sorts with the Vatican, possibly because at least two of the people who helped shape his ideas had been Catholic novices in their younger years. In *Mein Kampf* he modestly states 'And so I believe that my conduct is in accordance with the will of the Almighty Creator. In standing guard against the Jew I am defending the handiwork of the Lord'. He even failed to add that, in any case, the Almighty would be with him in taking a dim view of the race that was instrumental in having Jesus crucified, possibly because this might have drawn attention to the fact that Jesus actually was a Jew.

Surprisingly Hitler also failed to make capital out of the fact that his anti-semitic policy was in accordance with that put forward in the sixteenth century by Martin Luther, who admonished his followers to emulate the common sense of other nations and eject the Jews from their country forever, after subjecting them to a variety of punishments such as setting fire to their synagogues or schools, taking all treasure of gold and silver from them, etc. All these suggestions were eventually adopted by the Nazi regime, with Madagascar and Palestine initially proposed as two possible destinations for the deportees. Going even further back, Hitler might have mentioned the expulsion of the Jews from England by King Edward I in 1290.

On the other hand the ethical stance of *Mein Kampf* throughout veers starkly away from Christianity, yet neither the German Churches nor the Vatican commented on this. The principal message of the book was, after all, that nature shows us that the fittest survive to carry on the race, and it is the sacred duty of all Aryans to ensure this by subjugating inferior races by all available means. For the Germans in particular, this meant acquiring more 'Lebensraum' (living space) so that 'our people may be enabled to fulfil the mission assigned to it by the Creator'. There is no doubt here that Hitler believed that it was in fact the German race and not the Jews who were 'the Chosen Race'.

Fuelled by Hitler's heroic vision of German knights wielding their swords to conquer land needed by the German peasants to grow food for the German people, as embodied in his recurring phrase 'blood and soil', *Mein Kampf* throughout portrays the Jews as the arch enemies of the German people. They were, after all, the propagators of both Marxism and Capitalism (a most unlikely combination). They were followed, on the scale of his abhorrence, by the Social Democrats, with bourgeois intellectuals, homosexuals and pacifists bringing up the rear. Hitler's on-going admonishment was to show no mercy to these sub-humans, and to use all available means, including propaganda, whether true or not, to achieve the triumph of the Aryan race.

With some undoubted impetus due to the rise of the National Socialist Party, but not a likely cause of it, *Mein Kampf* eventually sold well and made Hitler a small fortune by the time he became Chancellor in the Reichstag elections in 1933. It also continued to contribute to the Nazi coffers when it was 'given' as a free, but state subsidized, wedding gift to all, except of course Jewish couples. The person who had assisted in the editing, and some have even claimed the writing of the book, one Bernhard Stempfle, happened to be another ex-Catholic novice (like the abovementioned Lanz von Liebenfels) and also editor of a rabidly anti-semitic newspaper.

In 1935, ten years after the publication of *Mein Kampf*, Irene Harand, a Catholic Viennese anti-Nazi campaigner, published a book under the title *Sein Kampf* ('His Fight'), with the subtitle *The Answer to Hitler from Irene Harand* [28]. She managed within just 250 pages, using quotations from a variety of prior authorities on the subject, to effectively demolish the anti-semitic racist theories of *Mein Kampf*, in addition to showing Hitler up as a deranged rabble rouser. She also accurately forecast what would happen if the world failed to take immediate action to squash Hitler's territorial ambitions. Tragically, by another accident of history, the book appeared too late, and its effect was lost in the rising tide leading up to the Anschluss in Austria. Nevertheless Irene Harand was put on the Third Reich's 'hit' list, but happened to be visiting England at the time. She went on to America and continued her anti-Nazi campaign there until America came into the war. It was not until 1969, however, that she received recognition for her work both from Israel and her native Vienna. Her Jewish fellow campaigner, the lawyer Moriz Zalman, was less fortunate, and died in Sachsenhausen concentration camp in 1940.

In spite of *Mein Kampf* the Nazi party had little influence until the German economy was hit by the Great Depression, another accident of history which helped Hitler to power. It resulted in the Nazi's share of the votes in the Reichstag elections rising from 2.6% to 33.1% in the four years ending November 1932, the month of the last democratic elections in Germany until after the war. This in turn led up to the next significant accident of history, the forming of a the coalition of the Nazi party with the other right wing parties of the old school, who believed that by supporting Hitler's promotion to Chancellor they were just filling a temporary gap until a man of their own choosing could be found. As the historian Alan Bullock put it, 'Far from being inevitable, Hitler's success owed everything to luck and the bad judgement of his political opponents and rivals.'

Bad judgement in this case turned out to be catastrophically bad, since the man they considered insignificant and relatively harmless was, to all intents and purposes, a psychotic. As he himself states in *Mein Kampf*, he never had to revise or change anything he had learned about the world in general and the Jews in particular during his time in Vienna. His ideas about the significance of race then were almost identical to, and probably partly acquired from Lanz von Liebenfels, who was described by his psychologist biographer as 'estranged from reality and undoubtedly pathological'.

And so Hitler found himself on the crest of the wave. The picture of him sitting next to Hindenburg at his inauguration as chancellor shows him still kowtowing to the establishment, looking ill at ease and out of place in his pin-stripe suit – one of his last public appearances not dressed in uniform. Hitler's on-going theme of 'blood and earth', symbolising the need for wars of conquest to gain earth (often referred to as 'Lebensraum', i.e. 'living space' in the Nazi press) for sustaining the growth of the master race, was reflected in his style of apparel for publicity photographs. Produced by his own resident photographer, they show him alternating between his military breeches and brown shirt, symbolising his association with his heroic Siegfried (blood), and his leather shorts to symbolise him as the tiller of the soil (earth). It is worth noting that the latter attire became less frequent after his rise to power, no doubt influenced by the fact that he now moved in circles where tilling of the soil was regarded as a socially inferior occupation.

In addition to that, Hitler's approach to the 'personality cult' was ahead of its time, though the 'mass of the people' he liked to appeal to has not changed much since Roman times in its need to idolize a person rather than an idea.

What came after his election as Chancellor, as they say, is history. A reckless opportunist, Hitler immediately took steps to deal with his parliamentary opposition by outlawing their parties and putting the leaders of Communist, Social Democratic parties and Trades Unions in concentration camps specially set up for this purpose, on the pretext that their policies were subservient to the evil communist regime in Russia. His Brownshirt army, after years of street fighting with the communists, were well equipped to help enforce these activities, and within two years Hitler had relegated the Reichstag to a powerless advisory body. By the time his right-wing coalition partners had come to realise their mistake, it was too late, and not long after that Hitler began an on-going career of murdering those who got in his way.

This change in character from relatively harmless rabble-rouser to initiator of murder on an increasingly large scale can also be attributed to his meteoric rise to power, which had confirmed his growing delusion to be right in everything he did to an unfathomable extent (hence Ian Kershaw's choice of title for his book *Hitler 1889-1936: hubris* [29]). From then on Hitler was prepared to do anything to safeguard his success, even if it meant murdering his one-time associates. Thus, although throughout his rise to power he had maintained a good relationship with his principal early supporters, and even put up with Jews associated with members of his entourage or of the German cultural establishment, he made an immediate start on his subsequent career as a mass murderer by ordering the execution of his one-time friend and supporter Roehm.

Roehm was the leader of Hitler's Brownshirt army, also known as the SA ('Sturm Abteilung', i.e. 'Storm Division') which had helped him in his rise to power. When its public image became tainted by its unruly behaviour, sometimes even involving homosexual orgies, and Roehm had let it be known that he regarded his SA as the future German Army, Hitler realised that he was about to lose the support of the German military establishment, which would have jeopardized the future of the Nazi Party as well as his own. With Himmler's help he arranged Roehm's execution together with that of his principal followers, resulting in some 200 assassinations in what became known as the 'night of the long knives'.

It was the first time the ex-German Army corporal had resorted to murder when confronted with a challenge to his authority, to be followed by numerous other occasions after the laws of the Third Reich had been amended to make any form of opposition to Nazi policy punishable by death. In this instance, however, he was still required to offer an explanation to the Reichstag, which he did, with the aid of the Goebbels–controlled media, explaining that his victims had betrayed National Socialism in particular and the German people in general, thus endangering the future of the Third Reich.

Hitler here gave an intimation of things to come, and of how his increasing anger at any opposition, a common symptom of the mentally unstable, led to his ruthless suppression of it, together with the continual repetition of his order to his followers that they must show no mercy in the face of an enemy intent on destroying the German people. Whether, as was rumoured over the years, he ever actually bit the carpet in his recurrent rages, has not been documented. What did soon become evident, however, was his increasing self-assurance over those years. This was particularly noticeable at the Nazi rallies, when, prior to beginning his speeches addressing some 20,000 or more of his followers, his pauses waiting for complete silence before launching himself grew longer and longer over the years – a far cry from when he first harangued his fellow workers on a Viennese building site to the point where they threw him off the site.

The next accident of history which helped Hitler considerably in his quest to assume absolute power was his association with the gifted German film producer Leni Riefenstahl, who agreed to film the 1934 Nuremberg rally, when some 700,000 members of the SA and the SS paraded to affirm their support of the Fuehrer, as he had already become known. Leni Riefenstahl used ground-breaking techniques in the making of the film, 'The Triumph of the Will', which has been acclaimed to this day as a masterpiece of documentary film-making. The title, devised by Hitler himself, was meant to imply that it was his willpower that had brought the Nazi party to power. Two years later Riefenstahl made a film of the 1936 Berlin Olympics, which after its release in 1938 added to the international recognition of the Third Reich

Although he was reputedly the originator of 'the final solution', exactly what this was to be at the time has never been established. There is certainly no intimation of it in *Mein Kampf*. If there had been, he would have been ostracised as a dangerous lunatic. The only intimation of any plans for the German Jews, mooted numerous times right up to the beginning of the German invasion of the USSR, was to re-settle them outside the German Reich. After the beginning of the war this plan became less likely to be implemented (though a deportation to Palestine actually took place) since the proposed destinations were no longer practicable, and were replaced by schemes for resettlements in the newly conquered territories of Poland and the Ukraine, eventually extending to Siberia. It was only after none of these options remained viable alternatives that the Gauleiters in Poland, faced with ever increasing numbers of Jewish deportees to accommodate, took matters into their own hands by authorizing the shooting and gassing of trainloads of Jewish deportees from Germany, Austria and the German occupied territories. This was later followed by the gassing of those already in concentration camps who were no longer physically able to contribute anything to the war effort.

Precisely when Hitler himself decided to make extermination of the Jews his ultimate aim has never been established, but, as Steven Pinker observes in his *The Better Angels of Our Nature*[30], there is no indication that anyone but Hitler and a few fanatical henchmen thought it was a good idea. Judging by his comment 'who, after all, still speaks today of the extermination of the Armenians', we are justified in thinking Hitler would not have had any qualms of following this relatively recent example of a genocide.

Throughout the remainder of his career as 'the Fuehrer', Hitler left the day-to-day running of the Reich to his associates and minions, and only dealt with major political decisions and military strategy himself. Initially the Wehrmacht Generals regarded the latter as either reckless or deranged, starting with the remilitarization of the Rhineland, and continuing through the annexation of Austria and the Sudetenland right up to the invasions of Poland and France. In every case the German military establishment had to eat humble pie, principally because the British and French had thought, exactly as they had, that no sane leader would take such risks. What they had all overlooked was that he was, if not insane, at least deranged. As a result, the Generals had little option but to continue to go along with Hitler, who made sure their subservience was rewarded by salaries and pensions which not many would have been able to resist. His initial successes in proving his generals' reservations about his reckless strategy wrong bolstered his delusion considerably, as shown by a throwaway statement quoted by his secretary, Traudl Junge, in *Until the Final Hour.* She was referring to one of his usual cosy mealtime gatherings with his (mostly female) staff at his Berghof Residence at Berchtesgaden, when he explained his reasons for not having children (with Eva Braun). These were based on the consideration that men of genius don't have time to devote to fatherhood, and in any event their children never measure up to their fathers. Traudl Jung was used to references by the Fuehrer to his mission in life having been decided by a higher providence (i.e. God), but his confession to being a genius made her realise the extent of his megalomania.

Although the author of *Mein Kampf* was never short of a rant on any subject to do with his own pet hates, none of his verbose statements would entitle him to be ranked as a great thinker. Open *Mein Kampf* on any page, and the probability is that it will contain several statements which are either untrue, debatable or ridiculous, or all of these, as for example the following: 'But in North America the Teutonic element, which has kept its racial stock pure and did not mix it with other racial stock, has come to dominate the American Continent and will remain master of it as long as that element does not fall a victim to the habit of adulterating its blood.'

When finally face to face with reality during his last days at the Berlin Chancellery, with the Russian army almost at the door, Hitler blamed the German people's weakness for its downfall. One can only conjecture how the course of history would have changed had Hitler's application to join the German army in Munich in 1914 been rejected. Very likely he would have followed in the footsteps of his one-time guru, Lanz von Liebenfels, and started his own version of 'The New Temple' in Munich, eventually to disappear from public view as his guru did. His life was a historical accident and, like any tornado or earthquake, had similar devastating results on its human victims. Any final judgement of him as a human being, however, has to take account of the extenuating circumstance that he was himself a victim of his own delusions.

Next in line to Hitler in the scale of evil would undoubtedly be Himmler. Although unlike his Fuehrer by nature withdrawn and not subject to uncontrollable fits of anger, he came closest to him in his hatred of the Jews. He did more than any of Hitler's other followers to go some way towards making the Fuehrer's vision of a 'Jew-free' Germany followed by a 'Jew-free' Europe a reality. Yet there was nothing in his middle-class upbringing or family life which could have given a clue to the cause of his fanatical hatred of the Jews, and eventual abandonment of his Catholic beliefs. He was never a good mixer, probably because from the start he developed an introspective personality. Although physically quite remote from the ideal version of Germanic manhood, and, unlike his siblings, not good at sports, he was already full of patriotic fervour in his teens, and after some preliminary military training just failed to see service at the end of the first world war. After a spell at the Munich Technical College studying agronomy, he was working as a farm manager when he was first recruited into the Nazi party. He soon became an ardent follower of the Fuehrer, who had noted the organisational skills behind the unattractive façade, and he remained a willing tool in Hitler's increasingly ruthless treatment of the Jews in his capacity of SS supremo.

Himmler was not known to be brutal in his personal life, either with his family, his associates or subordinates. But he was a secret schemer and manipulator, with a fanatical belief in the German Teutonic mythology and its mission in the world. During the years leading up to the war he personally instigated and helped to finance expeditions around the world to establish evidence of a Teutonic civilisation preceding Christianity, eventually even tracking down what his researchers claimed was the location of Parsifal's Holy Grail.

He became responsible for the training and engagement of the SS Einsatz commandos in the 'cleaning up' of the civilian populations behind the army front lines, which in the case of Poland meant all Jews, communists and resistance fighters, plus all aristocracy and intelligentsia who might have become a focus of resistance.

Himmler was also the architect of the final solution through the setting up of the gas chambers at Auschwitz. He was not the originator, but certainly the enabler of the Holocaust, in his role of head of the SS. Even he, however, had had doubts when Hitler first intimated to him a 'Final Solution' of the Jewish problem, i.e.

mass murder. His reservation, as recorded in his diary, was simply that he considered it 'un-German' since it did not fit in with his idea of German heroic mythology. However, after due reflection, and no doubt influenced by his abject subservience to the Fuehrer's ideas, it did not take long for him to change his mind.

He then went to work enabling Hitler's idea, and it was not long before he had recruited a team, including Heydrich, to make it all happen, and the details were hammered out at the infamous 'Wannsee' conference in Berlin.. Throughout this he instilled his select team with the importance of secrecy for this project, and that only those of great strength of character should be selected to carry it through, since those that weakened at the sight of mass executions could become a danger to the future of the 'Thousand Year Reich'. Furthermore, they should ensure that all those who took the oath of secrecy should be told that breaking this for whatever reason would make them liable to instant execution. As mentioned in Breitman's *The Architect of Genocide*[15], there was in fact a report of two executions for careless talk within a month of the beginning of the gassings.

So both Hitler and Himmler were well aware that they would never be able to gain the support of the German nation for the final solution, and this, above all other reasons, is why the bulk of the German people knew nothing about the holocaust until after the war.

Amongst the remainder of Hitler's close followers the ranking for epitomes of evil is not as clear-cut, but would roughly be graded in a diminishing order of Goering, Goebbels, Bormann, Hess and Speer, the last two being the only ones not sentenced to death at Nuremberg. It is however unlikely that any of these would have supported the genocide, although both Goering's and Goebbels' racist fanaticism fell not far short of Hitler's or Himmler's.

Of middle-to upper-class Prussian origin, Goering had become an air ace in the first world war in the wake of von Richthofen, which helped to set him on a course of becoming a heroic figure in keeping with his Wagnerian world view of the Germanic knights. After being wounded by a bullet during the coup of 1923, he had escaped from Munich to his wife's home in Sweden. He was later pardoned by the German Government and returned to Germany in 1927. After a rapid rise from car salesman in Berlin to president of the Reichstag, he eventually became chief of the Luftwaffe and Reichsmarshall. The hunting lodge named Carinhall after his first wife, built on an estate some 80km north of Berlin, was later used by the Nazi top brass for entertaining important visitors, and eventually blown up by Goering himself before the Russian army could get to it, perhaps acting out the end of 'Goetterdaemmerung' (Twilight of the Gods), the last opera in Wagner's Nibelungen Ring Cycle.

Unlike Goering, the rest of Hitler's minions were, like him, of lower middle class origin. Goebbels started working life as a reporter on a minor newspaper, and came to prominence together with Hitler as his propaganda chief. Although already a rabid anti-Semite from the start of his career, his racist beliefs were bolstered by his meeting with Houston Chamberlain at Bayreuth, where he was attending a Wagner opera production together with Hitler.

After the Nazis came to power, and following Hitler's lead, Goebbels had also turned on his old comrades in the SA, and supported Hitler's orders to execute the ringleaders when they were considered a potential threat to the popular image of the Nazi party.

Goebbels used his propaganda skills through Nazi newspapers relentlessly from the beginning. The success of Leni Riefenstahl's films made him realise the importance of this medium. Of the numerous subsequent wartime films produced at Goebbels's personal instigation, two proved to be particularly successful in reviving lagging support for the regime. One was 'Ohm Krueger', a supposedly biographical film about the South African Boer leader which portrayed the young Churchill as a ruthless Concentration Camp commandant, and made the point that it was the British who had first used this method of detaining opponents of their regime. Another film, aimed principally at the German public was a new version of 'Jew Suess', based on the novel by Lion Feuchtwanger under the same title. This had previously been filmed in Britain in 1934, with the German refugee film star Conrad Veidt in the title role. Goebbels's version, needless to say, distorted the book's portrayal of the tragic figure of Suess into that of an evil scheming crook, to help revive sagging anti-semitism

Goebbels remained loyal to his Fuehrer till the end, and committed suicide with his wife in the bunker in Berlin, after having his children killed with lethal injections.

Hitler's private secretary and assistant Martin Bormann, like Goebbels, was under Hitler's sway from the start. Again of lower middle class origins, he had early on acquired experience of managing people as a farm manager, and became particularly adept at doing so as Hitler's secretary. His principal function was to work behind the scenes, organising both people and money on an ever increasing scale. He finally became Hitler's intermediary with the real world to the extent where it was likely that Hitler's orders were actually Bormann's. He was largely instrumental in the development of the mountain retreat at Berchtesgaden, where he had managed to raise huge amounts of money in order to comply with Hitler's merest whims, in addition to building a residence for his own family there. He was also adept at giving hand-outs to all in Hitler's immediate entourage in order to assure their cooperation or, more often in later years, their compliance. Like Goebbels, he also remained loyal to the Fuehrer till the end, and was killed during his escape from the bunker in Berlin.

Rudolph Hess, Hitler's first personal assistant and later Deputy Fuehrer, was somewhat overshadowed by Himmler in later years. A loyal and fervent follower of Hitler, his intellectual powers were modest, to the extent that he convinced himself that he would be able to broker a peace deal with the Earl of Hamilton based on a very brief acquaintance. His flight to England in 1940 and subsequent imprisonment was enough to enable Hitler to brand him a madman. Many years after his committal to serve his life-sentence in Spandau prison, he claimed that his defence at the

Nuremberg Trials that he had lost his memory was a lie. If so, it helped to save his life. In the end, he chose to terminate it himself at the ripe age of 93.

Albert Speer, Hitler's architect and eventually Minister of Armaments and War Production Chief, was perhaps the most intelligent and cultured of Hitler's associates. He first came to Hitler's notice when he engaged him to produce some architectural drawings of his various grandiose plans for Nuremberg and Berlin. Already a member of the party, Speer at first declined any fees for these services, which alone showed him to be at least not mendacious, unlike many others in Hitler's entourage. One of his principal contributions in the early years was the layout of the Nuremberg stadium, coupled with his idea of using some 130 anti-aircraft searchlights borrowed from the Wehrmacht to provide a dramatic night-time backdrop to the Nuremberg rallies, all duly immortalized in Leni Riefenstahl's film. In his later capacity of Armaments Supremo he was responsible for the transportation and use of millions of slave labourers throughout occupied Europe. He finally blotted his copybook with Hitler by secretly contravening his instructions to destroy all factories, bridges and railways about to fall into the hands of the Red Army in order to safeguard at least a remnant of a future for the survivors. At their last meeting in the Berlin bunker he admitted this to Hitler. By this time it was too late for any action to be taken against him, and Hitler was in any event too weak to have him arrested.

Speer was one of the few to plead guilty to complicity to war crimes at Nuremberg, but never admitted to knowing anything about the gas chambers. He wrote several books of memoirs during his twenty year confinement at Spandau. In her biography of him Gitta Sereny describes numerous unsuccessful attempts to get him to rescind his claim of ignorance of the final solution.

Another example of extreme evil would be Franz Stangl, the Austrian commandant of Treblinka for a year. By his association with Treblinka alone, he would qualify for the epitome of all evil committed by the Nazis with the gas chambers. Closer inspection, however, reveals a number of extenuating circumstances leading to his involvement. Whilst still in the Austrian Police, he had offended the Nazis (then an 'underground' movement in Austria) by uncovering a Nazi arms cache in the forest in his area of Austria, an action which earned him an Austrian police medal. After the Anschluss this immediately became a threat hanging over his head, and was eventually instrumental in his accepting a position in charge of security with 'the General Foundation for Institutional Care'. The name of this Foundation was really a Euphemism for euthanasia carried out by means of gassing or lethal injections of selected inmates of institutions for the insane or severely deformed at a number of secret locations in Germany and Austria. Stangl later claimed he had been told by one of the Nazi health officials that he need not have any moral concerns about engaging in this activity, since euthanasia of this kind was already practised in America and Russia.

The establishments engaging in this activity were eventually closed down when information regarding them had leaked into the public domain and provoked outrage from the religious establishments. By that time, however, the bulk of the organisation's initial target had been met, to a total of some 50,000 individuals, a large proportion of these being children.

As Stangl told his interviewer during his eventual trial in Germany, his function at the Foundation had been merely to ensure that strict guidelines were followed in the selection of the potential victims of 'hospitalization', the euphemism employed in order to keep the euthanasia procedures secret. He mentioned one occasion when he had incurred the displeasure of the Mother Superior at a home for the disabled, by having to inform her that a candidate for euthanasia put forward by her did not meet the required criteria.

After the abandonment of the euthanasia programme Stangl was offered a position at Treblinka. When he found out this was really an extermination camp, he asked to be allowed to choose another posting instead, only to be told by his future boss that he was already a party to a top secret activity, and his refusal to accept the position would jeopardize his career, and possibly his life. Stangl complied, both in the interests of his survival and that of his family, and applied his organisational skills to the efficient running of Treblinka. In the first instance, this involved creating order in the camp, which was run by a dissolute gang of SS personnel. The actual procedure consisted of herding the prospective victims into the gas chambers under the pretext that they were there to take a shower, having first stripped them of all clothing, cash and valuables. The disposing of the corpses after the event was left to the camp slave labourers, leaving the SS to help themselves to the heaps of accrued paper money to pay for prostitutes from Warsaw bordellos to entertain them.

Stangl soon put a stop to that, and ensured that all the accumulating wealth would go directly to his superiors at Lublin, and hence to the Reich's financial institutions, where it would be used to help the war effort by financing the purchase of badly needed Swedish steel amongst other necessities.

Stangl claimed that he himself was never anti-Jewish, and that his superiors were principally motivated by the urgent need to finance the war effort. According to Gitta Sereny in her book *Into that Darkness*[30] the total amounts gathered from the death camps came to just short of 800 million Reichsmark.

The operation at Treblinka was terminated a year after it came into operation. After the end of the war Stangl escaped to South America and was able to get his wife and children, who had remained in Austria during his year at Treblinka, to join him there. Although he had never discussed his work at Treblinka with his wife, a devout Catholic, she did in the end succeed in getting him to tell her. She was distraught, but decided she had to live with it, as he had.

At the end of Gitta Sereny's odyssey *Into that Darkness*[31] to explain the mentality of Stangl, she finally succeeds in getting him to admit to feeling guilt for not having chosen to sacrifice himself and his family rather than engage in his appointed task. By that time Stangl had already served six months of the life imprisonment sentence passed on him at the end of 1970 by the War Crimes

Tribunal, but his punishment was short-lived since he died of natural causes the day after Sereny's last interview with him.

Another 'epitome of evil' is Adolf Eichmann, who only achieved prominence after being kidnapped in Argentina after the war and taken to Jerusalem for trial by Israeli agents. His role at the beginning of the war had been that of organising the forced emigration of the Jews from Austria, and preparing plans for their complete removal from the greater Reich after the war, possibly to Madagascar. These were the heady days of 1940 when a speedy conclusion to the war was expected by Hitler and his entourage. Eichmann was then also involved in the arrangements for transporting three liner loads of Jewish refugees from Romania to Palestine, where they were refused entry, with the British High Commission ordering the refugees to be taken on to Mauritius.

The turning point for Eichmann came when Heydrich, his boss, conveyed to him the plans for 'the final solution' in the late summer of 1941. As from that date, the removal of the Jews from the Greater Reich was to be prosecuted with no holds barred. This meant that instead of sending them to the already overcrowded ghettos in Poland, those of them that could not be usefully employed in the war machine would simply be murdered by means still to be finalised.

Eichmann later claimed that he was horrified at the idea, but wisely refrained from letting Heydrich know about this. In the final years of the war he was responsible for the efficient removal of the Jews from all the conquered territories to labour and/or extermination centres at Auschwitz, Treblinka etc, and spent some time in Hungary dealing with necessary arrangements for deportations there. His principal ethic in life was obedience to his superiors, and doing his work to the very best of his abilities. The two occasions when he was actually called upon to witness the end result of his activities, i.e. gassings and shootings, he felt unable to watch.

Eichmann was never a 'big shot' in the holocaust machine, just a cog. After the end of the war he escaped from detention in Germany, and with the aid of the Vatican's 'Pontifical Commission of Assistance' aimed at helping anti-communist refugees to emigrate, he managed to get to Argentina in 1950, and made a life for himself and his family in Buenos Aires. Unlike some of his former SS senior colleagues there, he did not become wealthy and successful, though he had managed with the aid of his sons to build a family house in a remote suburb of Buenos Aires, within a bus journey of where he worked at the Mercedes-Benz factory as a welder. It was after arrival at his home bus-stop at the end of a working day in May 1960 that he was kidnapped by the Israeli Mossad agents and taken to Jerusalem for trial.

The assessments of Eichmann and his trial in Jerusalem, such as Hannah Arendt's *Eichmann in Jerusalem* (1963) and the much later *Eichmann – His Life and Crimes* (2004) by David Cesarani differ significantly in their view of the 'evil' in the man. His anti-Semitism by the latter years of the war is not questioned by either author, but that could hardly be the basis of a judgement of him being evil per se in the context of what was going on in Hungary, Slovakia and Bulgaria, where the mass deportations of Jews were in full swing with no significant opposition, and sometimes even support, from the general public and the Churches. Whatever the arguments of the prosecution case were, the predictable death penalty aroused a mass of protest from the Western intelligentsia, ranging from Victor Gollancz, Arnold Toynbee, Bertrand Russell, Richard Crossman, Arthur Koestler and Pearl Buck, two of whom were Jews themselves. They regarded it as an act of vengeance, made farcical by the fact that thousands who had been more directly involved in the Holocaust than Eichmann were left untouched, many of them living opulent lives in both South and North America.

Although it has become universally acceptable to describe Hitler as the ultimate evil, he did no more than convince a small nucleus of his followers that it was necessary and commendable to kill those who opposed his notions of what God had in mind for humanity in general and the German people in particular. In this respect he was no more evil than many of the Kings, Prophets and priests who also did just that from times immemorial onwards.

Unlike Hitler, his predecessors in the killing of opponents had no need to keep these activities secret, since they had the full support of the establishment, and in those days what the rest felt or thought about it did not count. This observation alone should provide us with the principal reason for elevating Hitler's deeds above those of his predecessors in terms of evil: he and his small band of executioners carried out their work in secret and without the approval of either the German establishment or the bulk of the German people.

Like their predecessors, Hitler and his followers were also victims of history. Due to their experiences in their formative years, they had developed exaggerated prejudices which made those who did not share these prejudices representatives of ultimate evil. The Jews, being at the top of their scale for evil, then also became victims of history. As for how we should have dealt with the perpetrators remains the subject of an on-going debate.

A lesser evil

The whole question of the morality of World War II, and indeed of any war, is one to which there can never be a conclusive answer. We, just like the Germans, were victims of history, and had no option but to try and stop Hitler and his gang of followers. Undoubtedly the persecution and eventual mass murder of a race was a greater evil than the killing of a much smaller number of people, many of whom were non-combatants, and some of whom might have condoned the former. But the escalation of brutality was engaged in by both sides in the war, in the case of the Allies principally with the bombing of civilian populations, to the extent that by the end of the war civilian casualties inflicted by us on the German population was in the order of ten to twenty times that inflicted by them on us.

In the beginning air attacks on Germany had been Britain's only available means of continuing the war. and these attacks had not been effective other than as morale boosters for Britain and irritants for the Germans. In August 1940, after German night bombers aiming for RAF airfields drifted off course and dropped bombs on London, Churchill ordered an immediate retaliatory raid on Berlin the following night. Goering, who at that time was already Air Marshall of the Luftwaffe, had to eat his words that if the British Air Force ever reached Berlin, he could be called 'Meyer' (a derisory term used by the Germans for idiots). Hitler was furious and ordered an immediate retaliation with interest, culminating in what became known as the 'Blitz' to Londoners. This again led to the escalation of the bombing of Germany by both the British and United States Air forces.

The historic image of Churchill as the saviour of Western democracies from the Nazi onslaught has stood the test of time, but has been tainted by some dissenting voices. Mahatma Gandhi, for instance, believed that Hitlerism and Churchillism were in fact the same thing, the only difference being one of degree. Of course he had good reason to dislike Churchill, who at one time had suggested that he 'ought to be laid, bound hand and foot, at the gates of Delhi and then trampled on by an enormous elephant' (see Richard Toye's *Churchill's Empire*[32]). This, according to Churchill at the time, would have been a solution to Britain's problems with (in his words), 'these beastly people with a beastly religion'. Neither was Hitler a fan of Gandhi, since he later proposed a less theatrical solution in the course of his discussions with Lord Halifax during the Munich negotiations, when he enquired why the British didn't just have Gandhi shot.

A closer inspection of Churchill's history and conduct of the war shows that in many respects both his world view and his actions were very similar to Hitler's. Like Hitler, Churchill had enjoyed World War I, and though conceding that it shattered the lives of thousands, confessed 'I enjoy every second of it.' Like Hitler, he abhorred Communism, and as Secretary of State for War in 1919 was instrumental in sending a British expeditionary force into Russia to assist the counter-revolutionaries. Although not anti-semitic per se, he was in the vanguard of those who saw a Jewish conspiracy to conquer the world, and went into print about it some five years before Hitler did so in 'Mein Kampf'. In an article in the London Illustrated Sunday Herald of Feb.8th 1920 he referred to 'The Protocols' (i.e. the Protocols of the Elders of Zion) and 'this sinister confederacy of international Jewry for the overthrow of civilization'. Like Hitler, Churchill associated Bolshevism with Jews because some of its leaders in Soviet Russia were Jewish. This, however, was by no means the principal reason for his abhorrence of communism per se, which was undoubtedly due to his aristocratic origins and upbringing. The eventual joining of forces with the Soviets was a difficult task for him.

After taking over the conduct of the war in 1940, he arranged for the immediate detention of all German nationals, regardless of whether or not they happened to be Jewish refugees. In 1944 he approved the deportation of some of the Austrian and German Jewish refugees who had arrived in Palestine illegally, having been taken there by three ships chartered by the German 'Committee for Sending Jews Overseas' under the supervision of Adolf Eichmann. In the event, Israeli agents mined the ship containing some of the refugees, with the idea of damaging it badly enough to prevent their further deportation. The mine, however, resulted in the loss of the lives of 260 deportees. Following an international campaign on their behalf, some of the survivors were finally permitted to stay in Palestine by the British government. Ironically, however, around a half of the original contingent was deported to Mauritius, not that far from Madagascar, Hitler's original destination for a Jewish colony.

One significant difference between Churchill and Hitler was that Hitler went to great lengths in his 'Mein Kampf' to convince the Germans that they were members of a superior race. Churchill had no need to do the same for the British, who already knew this to be the case.

Churchill's background was however completely different from Hitler's. His membership of the British aristocracy guaranteed his education at public school followed by Sandhurst, followed by a spree of various appointments in the British Empire, which at the time meant principally subjugating the inhabitants of places as diverse as South Africa, the Sudan, India and Australia. In his subsequent political career his racist postures rivalled Hitler's, as witnessed by his belief that the Aryan stock is bound to triumph, and that it was our duty to enforce our kind of civilisation on the backward peoples of the Empire (see *Churchill's Empire*[32]). His observations were, at times, more stringently and racially aggressive than Hitler's, such as 'there are less than seventy million malignant Huns (meaning Germans) – some of whom are curable and others killable.'

Hitler often exhorted all German soldiers to show no mercy, and to fight to the last man. Churchill didn't go quite as far, but also advised his Generals and Air Marshalls 'to show no mercy', and suggested that army officers should keep fighting until at least half their men were killed or wounded, an instruction one might consider difficult to follow 'on the ground'. Like Hitler, for every major air attack on his country he promised retaliation with interest, on an ever increasing scale.

Like Hitler with Houston Chamberlain, Churchill also adopted a guru, the German-born Professor Lindemann (see *Prof- the life of Frederic Lindemann*[33]). Later promoted to Lord Cherwell, Lindemann was an academic who had become known for his research in physics. His association with Churchill came about after he was appointed scientific advisor to the Government during the war, and they soon discovered that their views on racial supremacy coincided. If anything, Lindemann's views on inferior races extended to cover inferior classes as well, and particularly the working classes.

This may have influenced his commendation of the new policy of 'area bombing' to the Cabinet, which adopted it in 1942 with the ultimate aim of disrupting German war production by making the workers engaged in it homeless. Based on figures Lindemann had obtained from German bombing raids on Britain, he had estimated that for each ton of bombs dropped between 100 and 200 people would be made homeless, and estimated that if 58 of Germany's major cities were area bombed, this would amount to about a third of the country's 22 million urban population, i.e. over 7 million people. He gave no figures for the proportion of these 7 million likely to be made homeless forever because they had been killed in the process, nor how many were not workers themselves but their spouses and children, or even slave labourers and refugees, giving the impression that this information was not high on his agenda. By the time the policy of area bombing had been approved, adopted and extended to the use of incendiaries, the raid on Hamburg made 900,000 of its population homeless, in addition to incinerating some 45,000, i.e. 4.75% of those made homeless. If this percentage is applied to Lindemann's estimate of making some 7 million Germans homeles, it would have meant a total of over 330,000 deaths – not far off the actual figure achieved.

The war cabinet's revised bombing policy was criticised by George Bell, the then Bishop of Chichester who was not, however, supported by other church leaders. The Bishop of York, for example, openly stated in parliament that 'it is a lesser evil to bomb the war-loving Germans than to sacrifice the lives of our fellow countrymen'. The public was not officially informed of the change in strategy until the publication of 'The Strategic Air Offensive against Germany' by HM Stationery Office in 1961, i.e. nineteen years after the event, though war office reports on the bombing raids gave a good indication that 'the Huns' were being re-paid with interest.

It is worth noting, however, that the United States Army Air force was initially opposed to the British bombing policy of indiscriminate night time raids. It continued with its daytime precision raids in order to avoid killing German civilians even though this inevitably involved losing more of their aircrews.

The total number of German civilian deaths due to Allied bombing has since been estimated at between 300,000 and 600,000, the difference being due to the variety of factors used in the estimates, with an associated loss of some 87,000 Allied aircrew personnel. The images of bodies being laid out in German cities after the bombings are not that dissimilar from those of the stacks of concentration camp victims discovered at Buchenwald and Auschwitz at the end of the war – tit for tat, perhaps, or a lesser evil.

The change in British strategy, ably carried out by 'Bomber' Harris with the approval of Churchill, was motivated by the idea that the resulting pressure from the civilian workforce in Germany would result in the unconditional surrender demanded by the Allies. Post war analysis has shown this change in strategy to have had the opposite effect of stiffening resistance because of what the Germans saw as terror against the civilian population, even without Goebbels ceaselessly hammering home the point.

Churchill was no laggard when it came to showing no mercy to attain his desired ends, as witnessed by his personal minute to the Chiefs of staff in July 1944 when he suggested the use of poison gas to drench the cities of the Ruhr and many other cities in Germany, 'and if we do it, let us do it one hundred per cent'. In retrospect Churchill could also be seen as a role model for Saddam Hussein, whose method of dealing with difficult Kurdish tribes was to gas them. Perhaps he was just following in the wake of Churchill who, in his capacity of Secretary of State for War in 1920, contemplated the use of mustard gas against 'uncivilised tribes' in Iraq to encourage them to become more compliant to British rule. In his own words, 'I do not understand the squeamishness about the use of gas', and 'I am strongly in favour of using poison gas against uncivilised tribes. The moral effect would be so good that the loss of life would be reduced to a minimum.'

Nor had he been beyond authorising the sinking of a part of the French fleet anchored in a French-Algerian port after the capitulation of France with the loss of some 1200 French sailors. This took place after Admiral Darlan of the French Fleet had given him his word that he had issued an order that their ships must never be allowed to get into German hands, even if it meant scuttling them, which they eventually did with what remained of their fleet in Toulon. Although Churchill was devastated by the French casualty figures, he was pleasantly surprised by a rapturous approval from Parliament after the event.

Another policy advocated by Lindemann and initially supported by Churchill was the eponymous 'Morgenthau' plan devised by the U.S Treasury Secretary with the blessings of both Roosevelt and Stalin in 1943. Its principal aim was for the Allies to dismantle German industry after the war and convert the country into an agrarian economy. Goebbels used this widely publicised plan as an instrument to stiffen German civilian resistance, and it undoubtedly contributed to both the extension of the war and its associated casualties on both sides. Although the plan was criticised by Foreign Secretary Anthony Eden on the simple economic consideration that it would lead to massive unemployment and starvation in Germany, it was not finally abandoned until 1946.

'Showing no mercy' – the recurrent theme of both Hitler's and Churchill's instructions to their respective armed forces and in their public addresses, had first surfaced on the German side in 1902. Addressing his troops prior to their involvement in the quelling of the Boxer rebellion in China, Kaiser Wilhelm had advised them to 'emulate the Huns', thus being in fact the originator of the use (or more accurately misuse) of this term by Churchill many years later to describe the Germans. It is worth noting that the atrocities committed by the combined European and American expeditionary forces in terms of executions of the Boxers, combined with rape and looting of the civilian population, indicates that they had all followed the Kaiser's admonition.

Like Hitler, Churchill also felt the need to demonstrate his military acumen by telling his generals what to do, though with some more justification than Hitler. He had, after all, participated in the conduct of various military escapades during the first world war, though not always with great success, as illustrated by the failure of his Gallipoli campaign. In the Second World War he again liked to put his oar in, and tried to avert the establishment of a second front in France in favour of getting the Allied armies in Italy to cross the Alps into Southern Germany. He was overruled by Roosevelt, Eisenhower and Stalin, and. some military experts have since claimed that had his strategy been adopted, it would have prolonged the war considerably.

Siding with a lesser evil was a problem also encountered amongst the Allies in the war. At the Tehran Conference in late 1943, in the course of an after dinner discussion on how to deal with the Germans after the war, Stalin had put forward a figure of 50,000 to 100,000 Wehrmacht officers to be executed immediately and without trial. Roosevelt tried to make a joke of this by facetiously suggesting that he might consider a figure of 49,500, whilst Churchill, to his credit, went as far as vigorously opposing this suggestion. Stalin back-tracked, saying he was only joking, and the matter was left on the basis previously agreed, meaning that only those found guilty of war crimes should face execution..

Although Stalin's spurious suggestion was not agreed, the total number of people executed for war crimes and crimes against humanity was probably in excess of 100,000, and a good number of those were not tried before the sentence was carried out. All those executed as a result of Allied jurisdiction received a trial, with the exception of the Russian contingents that had fought for the Germans, who were forcibly repatriated after the war in accordance with what had been agreed with Stalin. These were no doubt dealt with summarily and without any form of trial in the Soviet manner of the day. As for the summary executions carried out in what had been German occupied territories after the end of official hostilities, including those of some death camp guards, we shall never know how many there were, but they were likely to have been at least in the tens of thousands..

The question uppermost in the minds of those engaged in and reporting on the Nuremberg war crime trials was to what extent individuals' knowledge of what was happening to the Jews during the war was a crime in itself, regardless of whether the individual concerned had any hand, directly or indirectly, in the implementation of these happenings. In the end the judges decided to limit the death penalty to those who had been directly involved, with those indirectly involved to be imprisoned for terms appropriate to the likely extent of 'what they knew'.

The Nuremberg trials have been extensively criticised in subsequent years, and have even been described as a farce, since at least some of the trials were conducted by judges appointed by the Soviet Union. Yet, in accordance with the definition of war crimes concocted for the trials, the Soviet Union should have been in the dock itself for the 1940 Talyn and other massacres of over 20,000 Polish officers, police and 'intelligentsia' initiated by the NKVD (People's Commissariat of Internal Affairs) and authorized by Stalin. This embarrassing piece of evidence, more so since the graves of the Polish officers were uncovered by the SS after the German attack on the Soviet Union, and widely publicised by Goebbels at the time, was studiously ignored by the Nuremberg judges, some of whom were in any case Soviets. Neither, of course, was the blanket fire- bombing of hundreds of thousands of German civilians ever considered a war crime, since again it would then have been necessary for the judges to indict their own employers. But, as Richard Overy comments in *The Bombing War*[34], 'the established rules for war, even for liberal democracies, were replaced by a moral expediency, and this extended well beyond the end of the war as far as the Nuremberg Trials.

Bringing the perpetrators of the Holocaust to justice would, on the face of it, appear to have been a reasonable and worthwhile undertaking, based on the idea that the punishment suffered by the perpetrators would serve as deterrent for others contemplating similar acts in the future. However, since the evil they perpetrated was in aid of what they believed, or had been led to believe, was a good cause which justified killing those opposed to it, they would not have been deterred by any mooted punishments, nor have those who have committed similar atrocities since. This consideration, i.e. the trial and execution of people for believing that killing people was acceptable for what they considered a good cause, inevitably results in the conundrum which faces all of those who engage in wars. Of course the trials could have demonstrated that what the accused believed in was immoral or deranged, or both, and confined the guilty in an institution until they accepted the error of their ways or were cured. By just perpetuating the killing, the judges did neither themselves nor posterity any favours.

A further observation on punishment for war crimes would be how and where to draw the line between the principal perpetrators and those who just obeyed orders, which would already have encompassed a considerable proportion of the German population, still leaving those who were just concerned with their own survival. The duty we impose on ourselves of punishing those who have committed evil acts as a deterrent for others remains, but can it ever be more than combatting evil with a lesser evil? As an extreme example to illustrate the problem we could look at the case of Stangl, the commandant of Treblinka. Should the Jewish slave labourers he employed to dispose of the corpses from the gas chambers have been tried themselves for assisting crimes against humanity? If not, the only reason for dealing more harshly with Stangl would be because the degree of duress he was under was less than that of his slave workers. They would have been shot on the spot for refusing to do what they were told. In Stangl's case, his refusal to take on the job of running Treblinka would, merely in view of his prior knowledge of it, have resulted in his quiet elimination by the SS, not to mention any likely consequences for his family in Austria.

Yet of the lesser epitomes of evil, like the ones eventually sentenced to death at the Nuremberg and subsequent war crime trials, very few would have been found to have any direct involvement with murder or brutality in any courts before or since. As many jurists have declared in later years, these trials were a farce, and the verdicts in large measure due to pressure from Soviet judges. They, after all, were simply adhering as far as possible to Stalin's view, already mentioned, that at least 50,000 of the top Wehrmacht officers should have been executed without any judicial considerations. One of the top Soviet judges, Iona Nikitchenko, was, after all, well used to complying with Stalin's wishes, having presided at Stalin's show trials in the pre-war years.

Most of those on trial, with the possible exception of Albert Speer, saw themselves in a rather different light, that of having been simply patriotic citizens who were fighting to free the world from the combined evils perpetrated by Jews and Bolsheviks. It is unlikely that any of them had either personally murdered anyone, or even given an order for anyone to be killed. Even Goering, who had signed the original request for Heydrich, Himmler's deputy, to devise a 'final solution' to the Jewish problem, claimed he did not know what this was to be.

Although complying with Hitler's policies for getting rid of Jews, communists and any other elements opposed to these policies by putting them into concentration camps initially in Germany and, after the beginning of the war, in the German occupied territories, none of the above had broken any international conventions. None were personally engaged in brutal acts, and their relations with those around them were no worse than what most would find reasonably civilised. Even the ultimate perpetrators, Hitler and Himmler, would fall into this category. The real problem arises when the question is asked as to how they could ever have believed that what they did was right.

The answer to this can only be that Hitler's lightening rise to power, and the military successes in the early years of the Blitzkrieg, all due to a number of unpredictable accidents of history, made them all believe he was infallible. A further escalation of Hitler's hubris was due to the fact that he survived twenty seven assassination attempts between 1934 and 1944, with only the last one resulting in minor personal injuries, the previous ones failing for numerous trivial reasons. Hitler's luck held out virtually until his end, but not that of his victims.

Finally, and more embarrassingly, comes the question of the lesser evil perpetrated by the Americans by their incendiary bombing of Tokyo and other cities with the aim of undermining the morale of the civilian population. The resulting death toll, mostly by incineration, was around 100,000, of whom the majority were not directly involved in the war. Not long after that, America succeeded in developing the atom bomb, culminating in its use on Hiroshima and Nagasaki, with an estimated additional mostly civilian loss of life of around 80,000 and 70,000 respectively, followed by another 50,000 who died of injuries or the effects of radiation in the months after the event. The total number of victims of both the fire and the nuclear bombings were then some 300,000, and that doesn't include those who died later due to the longer term effects of radiation. It could be argued that the Americans had achieved a higher killing rate than the Gas chambers and the Waffen SS combined.

One aspect of these mass killings which needs further comment particularly in its relevance to future wars is how to compare the individual guilt of those Germans who participated in the shooting and gassing of millions of their fellow humans

Houston Chamberlain – Hitler's guru.

Irene Harand who demolished 'Mein Kampf' with 'Sein Kampf'.

Hitler with Hindenburg after he was made Chancellor in 1933

Hitler in uniform – his Siegfried outfit

Hitler in leather shorts – tiller of the soil

Conrad Veidt in the film 'Jew Suss' made in 1934

Poster of the Nazi version made in 1941

Cut from Leni Riefenstahl's film 'Triumph of the Will' – Hitler at podium in foreground addressing over half a million storm troopers

Lindemann – Churchill's guru

Stalin, Rooseveldt and Churchill at Tehran 1943: Execute 50,000 to 100,000 German staff officers?

Mosley and his blackshirts

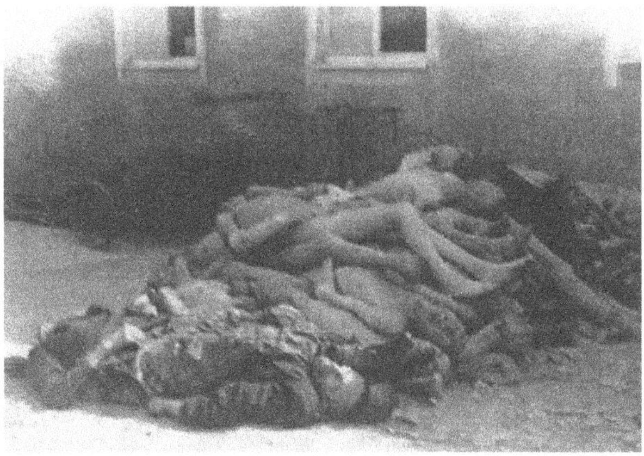

Victims of Nazi terror – bodies stacked outside Buchenwald after the liberation in 1945

Victims of Allied Terror – bodies laid out for identification after raid on Berlin in 1944

over a time span of several years with that of around ten American Aircrew incinerating and atomising a substantial part of a city population by simply pressing a button. In both cases the perpetrators acted to achieve what their superiors had assured them were desirable goals, since the victims belonged to an inhuman race. Ironically, at the time of the nuclear bombings in August 1945, the Nuremberg Trial prosecutors were preparing their case against the top Nazis for crimes against humanity.

The nuclear and fire bombings of Japan, however, have never been officially put into the category of war crimes. The people who made it possible were not punished but decorated. The simple moral yardstick was that the Japanese surrender ensured a cessation of the Allied losses involved had the war in the Pacific continued with the use of conventional weapons. This argument, however, ignores. the Japanese approach via Moscow to sue for peace, though not unconditionally, prior to the nuclear attacks. A post-war analysis has shown that the Japanese would have surrendered in any case had they known about the potential of the nuclear bombs. This does pose the question as to whether the Americans could have drastically reduced the scale of human suffering they perpetrated on the Japanese population by treating them as fellow humans rather than yellow devils. In the unlikely event that President Trueman had ever read 'Mein Kampf', he would have realised he was following Hitler's advice that 'the most cruel weapons are humane if they lead to victory'.

At a subsequent meeting with President Trueman, Henry Oppenheimer, the man in charge of the atomic bomb development at Los Alamos, commented 'we have blood on our hands'. Trueman told his Secretary of State never to let that cry-baby into his office again.

In view of the foregoing, we have to accept that even though we were waging a war against what we considered to be evil antagonists, we were also engaging in evil deeds, though on a lesser scale. We were fighting against what we considered to be an ultimate evil, but so were the Germans, the only difference being that they were mistaken in their choice. Herding people to dig their own graves before shooting them was evil, but so was releasing thousands of tons of incendiary bombs on cities like Hamburg, Dresden and Tokyo, to name but a few, followed by the atom bombs on Hiroshima and Nagasaki. The outcome in all cases was the same, but the victims of the fire- bombing or nuclear bombs might well have preferred being shot or gassed to being burnt alive.

The idea that the Germans were particularly prone to the attractions of Nazism due to their cultural traits is also suspect. What has to be considered is that National Socialism had its followers in Britain as well. Britain's own Nazi party started off as the 'Union of British Fascists and National Socialists'. Under the leadership of Sir Oswald Mosley, who has, like Hitler, been described as charismatic, it took off at a time when, as in Germany, the country was suffering from the Great Depression. Unlike Hitler, Mosley failed to get the necessary following from 'the masses' because he was seen by them as a member of the upper class, and when Germany became an evident threat to Britain, his support plummeted.

There were a number of other prominent figures in the British establishment in addition to Oswald Mosley who had fallen under Hitler's sway. Notably amongst the aristocracy was the Duke of Windsor, later to become Edward VIII, his paramour Mrs Simpson, Unity Mitford and her sister Nancy, Oswald Mosley's second wife. Then there were the press tycoons Lords Rothermere and Beaverbrook, together with a smattering of MPs. Rothermere had become an ardent Nazi supporter, and frequently used his Daily Mail to promulgate his views in that respect, even going as far as congratulating Hitler on his annexation of Czechoslovakia. Beaverbrook later joined him in appeasing Hitler's early transgressions until just before the beginning of the war, when both did a rapid about turn. Beaverbrook then went as far as advising us to 'cultivate a stern and righteous hatred of the Germans' and to 'also hate the Japanese- those barbarians who give us good cause for hate', and 'Now by hard and sharp blows and killing and killing it is time for us to show that we are the warriors of the world', just the sort of utterances we were familiar with coming from Hitler.

The reason why, unlike the Nazi Party in Germany, the British Blackshirts failed to make any impact on the population at large was that the British Union of Fascists never made an organised appeal to it with promises of jobs and a better standard of living, and continued to be viewed by it as a party of the establishment. It also failed to make an appeal to the anti-Semitic element, which would have given them the extra support they needed to emulate their German counterpart.

In *Soldaten – On Fighting, Killing and Dying*[35], the German Authors scrutinised and analysed secretly recorded conversations of German prisoners of war, many of which provided damning evidence of acts of brutality carried out by German soldiers. In spite of this, the authors' conclusions were that extreme violence was perpetrated by both sides, usually on an escalating 'tit for tat' scale. The shooting of prisoners, during or after their surrender, became commonplace, as witnessed by the account of the writer Ernest Hemingway of how he shot a captive German simply for having been a member of the Waffen SS, thus imitating what he believed would have been his victim's treatment of him had he been the prisoner.

What we failed to learn from the war.

The lesser evil perpetrated by the Allies at the behest of Churchill, Roosevelt, Trueman and Stalin, was in the end justified by putting an end to the greater evils perpetrated by Hitler and his followers. But many of the millions of victims on both sides need not have died had the Allied leaders been less intent on meeting brutality with brutality. The reason usually given, that this was the only message our opponents would understand, overlooked the fact that a 'message they could not understand' would have made a greater impact than one they could understand.

Very few in the post-war world had any doubts that what the Nazis did in the course of the war was of greater evil than what we did. The problem arises as soon as we accept that any means can be used to achieve the desired end, regardless of whether these are evil in themselves or not. Since war inevitably involves the killing of people, many of whom not associated with the evil we are intent on destroying, it can never do more than ensure the triumph of a lesser evil.

It was widely believed that most Germans had supported Hitler in his intent to destroy the Jewish race within the new boundaries of the Thousand Year Reich, and that they had some evil constituent in their genes prompting them in this enterprise. This would tacitly imply that Hitler had, after all, been right in attributing good and evil to race, he just got the race wrong. This is certainly a straightforward concept, and one that could have grown out of a belief prevalent in the early part of the 20th century that intelligence is related to race. If, however, the war was fought to prevent its perpetrators from realising their belief that some nations or races are intrinsically better or worse than others, it would imply that we didn't actually achieve this aim. At best, we failed to learn that we couldn't have this both ways. and that we have to accept that nations and races are all made up of a complete scale of good and evil, ranging from a the criminally insane and stupidly brutal, through the great majority who just do what they must to keep themselves and their family comfortable, to those who adhere to principles that go beyond this.

Most of the small minority of Germans or Austrians who had witnessed what was secretly being done in their name looked the other way, mainly in order to survive. We also tended to look the other way when we learnt that we were incinerating or atomising hundreds of thousands of 'others', even though our lives were not in jeopardy had we made a fuss about it. At worst we would have been socially ostracised. In any case, 'they' had started it all, so we felt justified, though secretly guilty.

Yet we felt morally superior to the Germans who, due to an accident of history, had become part of the killing machine before we did. Due to another accident of history, we had to make common cause with Stalin, who had already starved millions of his own people to death in what he considered to be a good cause, or a lesser evil. Yet not many have suggested we should feel ashamed for doing so. We have all unwittingly accepted the principle of supporting 'the lesser evil', and that the ends justify the means.

In later years, Gitta Sereny's interviews of Germans and Austrians involved or accused of war crimes describe her sometimes successful endeavours to get them to admit guilt, at least to themselves. She often used the phrase 'but they knew right from wrong, they just wouldn't admit that they hadn't had the courage to do the right thing'. This does raise the question how many of us, under the same circumstances, would have been prepared to die for 'doing the right thing'?

The whole question of 'Right and wrong', or let's just say morality, is in any case fraught with all sorts of imponderables. Few of the moral choices we have to make in everyday life have an answer that all of us, or even followers of any one religion or ethical belief system, can agree on. And even where we can agree that evil has been perpetrated, we still can't agree on how to punish the perpetrators. The debate about capital punishment worldwide is still on-going, with Western Europe the only continent which has finally abolished it.

Although Hitler and his immediate followers have gone down in history as epitomes of evil, they themselves were victims as well. They were conditioned by their upbringing and/or experiences to see the world in a different light from the rest of us. Like terrorists and suicide bombers, they were willing to give their lives for a cause they believed in, even though the rest of the world thought of it as being deranged. As for their followers amongst the wider populace, the punishment for the crimes against humanity they committed took no account of the extent of their just taking the easy way, nor of the brainwashing they had been subjected to by the Nazi propaganda machine. Yet it could be argued that in a civilised society we do not kill the deranged, we just confine them to where they can do no harm until such time as they can be regarded as cured.

Attributing regional, national or racial characteristics is a universal human activity, often connected with light-hearted but also often denigrating humorous anecdotes relating to foreigners. They mainly depict these as being either uncultured or at the least a bit odd. The terms most commonly used by the British when denigrating other national or ethnic groups include, frogs

(French, from frog eaters), Ities (Italians), Krauts (German, from cabbage eaters), gollywogs, wogs, niggers etc. (black people)

Few would go as far as to deny the existence of differences defined not just by regional accents but also behaviour. The problem arises when denigrating attributes of different groups are used to imply a moral superiority of one over another. Thus lumping the Germans, or even just those Germans who participated in the war, together into an evil race was not only irrational but also evil in itself by going along with Hitler's notion of 'blood' being a decisive factor in the 'good and evil' league. It was also dismissive of those hundreds of thousands of Germans who died in concentration camps or were executed for opposing Hitler.

One of the characteristics attributed to the Germans (mainly, I should add, by the British) is their lack of a sense of humour. Though not denying that there is a difference between the two, mainly in terms of kind and subtlety, to assert that the Germans don't have one is no more than a popular delusion of the British. Not just that, but the types of German humour vary with region just as they do in Britain. Berliner humour, in common with North German humour, has a certain brashness differentiating it from Bavarian humour. A typical example, based on personal experience, would be the following: English tourist question to a Berlin policeman – 'Excuse me, would you know where the Synagogue is?' Answer: 'Yes. Any other questions?'

Typical of the snide jokes about the Germans still prevalent to this day is the one that goes: 'Question: Why are German graves deeper than anyone else's? Answer: because deep down they're really quite nice'.To compound the view that all Germans were really involved in the Holocaust, we had adopted the notion that not only those alive at the time but their descendants should continue to be punished by reminding them of what their parents or grandparents had done. This notion, perhaps inspired by the biblical 'unto the third and fourth generation', apart from being more than a little out-dated, also ignores incidents in recent British history which should equally give us cause to feel guilt, such as the executions of participants in the Indian Mutiny in the 1850s, first use of concentration camps in the Boer War or the wholesale slaughter of civilians as a result of our wartime bombings.

Never again?

One significant factor in the establishment of the Nazi regime in Germany was the reluctance of its opponents to being thought 'unpatriotic' by criticising it at a time when it was seen to revive the economy and re-establish Germany as a power to be reckoned with. A power, moreover, which would see to it that it retrieved what the Treaty of Versailles had wrongfully taken from it. By the time they realised their mistake, if they were not already in concentration camps they knew that their only chance of remaining free was to keep their concerns to themselves.

Then, after the war had started, both those who heard just plausible rumours to those who had at least some reliable evidence of atrocities knew that keeping quiet was the price of survival. Their reaction was typically 'there's nothing we can do about it, so let's turn a blind eye'. A good example of this involved some of the executives of the company I.G.Farben which supplied Zyklon B gas supposedly for the control of vermin in concentration camps. They later found out that it was also being used for the control of what the Nazis would have referred to as 'bigger vermin'.

The basic instinct for survival also applied to those who were at far greater risk, such as the Jewish ghetto leaders who had to co-operate with the SS in policing their own people and helping them select those destined for deportation to the labour camps. At the time, fortunately, they were not aware that these were rapidly becoming transit camps to the gas chambers for those not able to work. Beyond that, Jews were eventually engaged in the orderly disposal of the bodies from the gas chambers, and also in maintaining discipline at the camps.

The Holocaust perpetrated by the Nazi Regime was not the greatest in history in terms of total numbers of people killed, but in terms of the rate of killings over the relatively short time span involved, i.e. around four years. Previous occurrences were simply associated with wars of conquest not governed by any rules of conduct such as the Geneva Convention, like the wave of Mongolians under Genghis Khan who swept across Europe in the 15th century, subsequent religious wars and pogroms such as the purges of the Armenians by the Turks in the 19th century.

Since the end of the war, there have been a whole series of genocides ranging from Bangladesh, Indonesia, Cambodia, Guatemala, Bosnia, Rwanda to the Sudan, all brought on by a clash of tribal and religious cultures. None of these, however, were perpetrated by a nation which had been at the forefront of Western Civilization. We have no reason to believe that there won't be repeats in the future, although it is highly unlikely that the Germans will be involved.

Some, but not many, historians might stick out their necks and give us a scenario of what the world might look like in a hundred years, principally because they wouldn't be alive to have to face any likely ridicule. A few might even engage in real risk taking and predict what is going to happen in the next five years. But if there is one thing history teaches us, it is that we never know what is around the corner, and even predicting what the world will be like in five years' time is a useless exercise. One good example of this was the lightening collapse of the former Soviet Union in 1991, just five years after President Reagan had committed the USA to the 'Strategic Defence Initiative', the Star Wars scenario fostered by what the American analysts saw as the increasing nuclear threat posed by the Soviets.

It has been postulated that the origins of a hurricane could be traced back, if that were possible, to the random flutter of a single butterfly's wings in some tropical forest. This would not be possible to prove even if assisted by the world's most advanced computers. Although all events happen in some sequential order, the conditions pertaining to each event are the result of an infinite number of circumstances. All natural catastrophes like hurricanes, tsunamis, earthquakes, volcanic eruptions, meteor strikes etc. are the result of a combination of events we cannot predict.

When it comes to human nature causing catastrophes for humanity, the random variables involved are also infinite. More than any other event in history, Hitler's lightening rise to power illustrates the ramifications of randomness. Many historians agree that if any one of the accidental events involving Hitler's career had not occurred where and when they did, there would have been no Holocaust. The same can be said about other human catastrophes brought on by individuals, ranging from Genghis Khan through Stalin to Mao Tse Tung.

One factor common to most conflagrations in the past has been the charismatic leader, religious, political or just born into the establishment, promising his followers a better future. In the case of the religious leaders, this promise was invariably only made to those who followed their god's commandments, and consisted of a life of eternal bliss in the hereafter. The avoidance of charismatic political leaders would seem to be a good guide for those wishing to avoid a repeat of the holocaust. Even modern democracies, however, are still at the mercy of the personality cult, with the result that our prime minister's score on that scale is more important than the policies he or she stands for. Although the man in the street likes to have someone to either identify with or hate, the idea that democracy should be dependent on one person's personality rating is outdated, and it is to be hoped that the next generation will veer away from it.

More important, however, is the avoidance of hunger and poverty in 'the masses', and excessive inequality between the richest and the poorest. Certainly both of these features were present prior to the toppling of existing regimes such as the Tsarist in Russia, Louis XVI in France, and the Weimar Republic in Germany.

Whether or not what happened in Germany after the Nazis took over will ever happen again on the same scale is just as unpredictable now as it was then. On the positive side, and in accordance to Steven Pinker's analysis of human conflict through the ages in his *The better angels of our nature*[30], the human race as a whole has become drastically less murderous in recent centuries in spite of the blip caused by the war. The optimism engendered by this work may have to be tempered by the universal acceptance of the notion that ethical standards are good in principle, but need only apply to 'us' if everyone else abides by them. This notion is particularly relevant in connection with the storage and deployment of nuclear weapons. Although international agreements putting a stop to further proliferation and the reduction of existing stockpiles are in force, they are being ignored with impunity. Invariably the arguments for doing so are 'well, they are not doing it, so we can't either'.' To put it another way, we only do the right thing once everybody else is doing it as well. The current argument for Britain retaining the nuclear 'Trident' submarine, is the more prosaic one that some 500 jobs are at stake.

There are, in addition, other considerations to be taken account of, such as those put forward by Eric Schlosser in his *Command and Control*[36] about the inherent risks in the current nuclear weapons deployment in the USA and worldwide. He analyses in detail the incident which had led to the explosion of a nuclear missile in its silo in an American missile launching pad, fortunately without actually detonating a nuclear explosion. This, in addition to numerous other near misses described by him, calls into question the accepted wisdom of Mutual Assured Destruction (MAD) by introducing the additional possibility of accidental self-destruction (ASD?)

Another point Schlosser makes is that although no rational world leader would contemplate a first strike, not all nuclear power leaders are known for their rationality, and he describes the current nuclear weapons distribution worldwide as a collective death wish. If it should ever happen, those who advocated MAD will presumably rest in peace knowing that they took at least the same number, and possibly more, of the opposite side with them. To those who argue that this was the only way of keeping the peace after Hiroshima, they can only mean the nuclear peace. As for the rest of human conflicts, they have gone on since, only slightly diminished but still resulting in untold millions of deaths.

Belonging

In the course of a lifetime of conflicting belonging I was frequently brought up short by the extent of its perseverance in our lives. One such occasion relates to my father, who had begun to suffer from dementure in advancing age. He was stayting with us in Dorset for a few weeks during which my mother was being treated for cancer in their local London Hospital. One day he had gone out of the house and disappeared. The Dorset police eventually tracked him down some miles from where we lived, having been apprehended by a kindly lady who took him in when he stopped by her house to enquire where he was. Realizing that he was confused, she contacted the police, who then brought him back to us. He was in a cheerful mood and became a gracious host to the two police constables who had returned him to us. He later responded to my question of where he thought he was wandering off to with 'You know your mother is in Berlin, so I just wanted to make some effort to go and see her there'!

My dual belonging has left an indelible imprint on my emotional and intellectual world view too. In later life I have retained a connection with Moedling through repeated return visits and contacts with my remaining friends and their relatives there up to the present day. Throughout my life I have often been questioned, and have questioned myself, about my compulsion to re-visit my childhood home town. I can only attempt an explanation by seeing my formative years as being an indelible part of me, as indeed they are for all of us. Christabel Bielenberg, the already mentioned author of the appropriately entitled *The Past is Myself*[20] about her experiences in Berlin before and during the war, knew this well. Beyond that, just seeing the houses and the trees and woods which remain after all those years, together with some of the people I had known then, and rekindling my memory of childhood events, offers me some solace for a happy childhood that is gone and yet lives on in my mind. Once again, an accident of history had played a part. My parents were catapulted into a life of sunshine, music and parties which were not dreamt of during their Berlin days. Not surprisingly, our years in Moedling have stayed with me as being happy, carefree and full of confidence in an even brighter future. Going back to the origins of these memories is perhaps an activity not all that different from visiting the grave of a loved one.

So Moedling has remained a recurrent landmark of 'belonging' throughout my life. For justification I feel bound to offer some tribute, which, like all our 'belongings,' is also bound to be prejudiced. My excuse for doing so is that, in my case, my prejudice is tempered by my additional belonging to another culture.

Moedling is now a satellite commuter suburb of Vienna, though technically still a town in its own right. Situated in a wine growing area nestled into the edge of the hilly slopes of the Vienna Woods on one side and facing the plains extending all the way into Hungary on the other, its history is littered with famous names. Beethoven composed the Missa Solemnis' and the 'Moedling Dances' here, the latter in what he referred to as the 'heavenly Bruehl', the valley which brings the Moedling stream out of the Vienna Woods. Schubert's 'Under the Linden Tree' was inspired by the same area, and Schoenberg, the inventor of the 12-tone scale, was a resident and many of his followers came there to 'learn the trade'. Other famous residents were Anton Wildgans, the acclaimed Austrian poet and playwright, and Franz Grillparzer, the dramatist and poet.

Then there is the Liechtenstein family, the original owners of Liechtenstein castle in Maria Enzersdorf, the adjacent village. Their descendants founded the principality of Liechtenstein and still own two palaces in the centre of Vienna today. Early in the 19thcentury Johann I. von Liechtenstein, engaged in a major landscaping of a part of the Vienna woods which contributed to the enduring charms of Moedling's environment. This relates principally to the introduction of the Black Pines prevalent in this region, together with the numerous restorations of historic remains.

Another connection of note that has only recently been established is the one with US Secretary of State John Kerry. It turned out that Moedling had been the home of Kerry's Jewish paternal grandparents. Kerry's grandfather, Fritz Kohn, went to school and was married here. Before emigrating to the United States in 1904, he decided to anglicise his name, which he reputedly did by closing his eyes in front of a map of Great Britain and lowering his index finger on what turned out to be County Kerry (now a part of the Republic of Ireland).

Moedling's historical landmarks consist of the St Othmar Church on the hill overlooking it, with its adjacent 'Charnel' tower which once contained the bones of the victims of the Turkish invasions of the 17th century. Further up the hill stands the

Black Tower, built by Count Liechtenstein over the remains of a previous fortification where the Turks had reputedly 'smoked out' the residents, with the adjacent 'Spectacle' arches looking out over Moedling towards the distant plains of Hungary. Bridging the entrance to the valley of the Moedling stream is the aqueduct which has been supplying Vienna with water from the 'Snow Mountains' further south since 1873. Another historical achievement associated with Moedling was the operation of the first electric tram-line in Europe, from the railway station to Hinterbruehl in the Vienna Woods. It had become defunct shortly before I arrived there in 1931, but the tramline rails were still there in the Schillerstrasse close to where we lived.

Further upstream of the Moedling brook Burg Moedling, the one-time home of the Babenbergers, the predecessors of the Habsburgs, dominates the valley, and beyond that, on another peak, the 'Hussar Temple' can be seen from afar. It was built by Count Johann Liechtenstein over the graves of five Hussars who died in the Battle of Aspern, the first time ever Napoleon was defeated.

A noteworthy feature of the town today, 85 years after its first opening, is the still magnificent indoor and outdoor swimming pool complex combined with winter skating rink, built in what at the time was still regarded as the revolutionary Bauhaus Art Nouveau style. As mentioned in the first part of the book, this had been the location of almost weekly visits for me and my family in my childhood, and it had close connections with both of my best friends' parents as well. With the stainless-steel and air-ventilated liner recently installed in its 50m outdoor basin it is probably still a European class leader, and a shining example of a local government sponsored enterprise. During my latter visits I was able to once again cast my eye over the painting of the nude lady in the indoor pool foyer which had made such an impression on my pre-pubescent mind, and can confirm that she still sports the black triangle between her legs which had attracted my attention then. Regrettably, I have to record that for a few years in the interim it was hidden by a bathing costume superimposed on the instructions of a sadly misguided Buergermeister.

Another important facet of Moedling dating back to my childhood and still going strong are the 'Heurigens', strictly meaning places licensed to sell locally grown 'this year's' wines, also providing local foods and sometimes 'Schrammel musik' (as originally composed and performed by the Schrammel brothers in the last quarter of the 19th century) to accompany their consumption. Less frequently now one still hears snatches of Viennese Music on the radio which brings back memories of a time when hardly a day went by without my hearing Viennese waltzes and excerpts from Strauss, Lehar and Kalman operettas. Among those that have stayed ineradicably in my mind are snatches from the 'The White Horse Inn', which accounted for my stay at the eponymous inn on Lake Wolfgang in 1948. This was eventually followed by my honeymoon there in 1953, when the first lines of the theme song: 'At the White Horse Inn on the Wolfgang Lake, there stands your luck at the door' was particularly appropriate. I witnessed a good example of the persistence of 'belonging' during a performance of this operetta at the Volkstheater in Vienna in 2009. When the character of the emperor Franz Joseph appeared on stage, sporadic clapping from the audience indicated that even then there were still some Austrians hankering after 'belonging' to the monarchy of the Habsburgs which had been abandoned some ninety years before.

Throughout my visits to Moedling over the years, I made attempts to find out what had happened to my Jewish school friends, invariably without success. Then, In 2007, I enquired at the local Museum what, if any, material they had in their archives to help me in my search. They couldn't offer me any information, but suggested I contact Frau Friederike Fida, a Vienna tourist guide resident in Moedling, who they knew had a personal interest in this topic. I arranged a meeting with her, and she quickly became an invaluable aide in my research.

One day, about three months after my first meeting with her, she sent me an e-mail to say she had tracked down a Dr.Roland Loewe in Vienna, and gave me his telephone number. A brief call (my first conversation with him after seventy years) confirmed his identity.

Roland had really been my brother Fred's friend, but I had also known him from visits to his home in Moedling together with Fred, at a time when his father, Dr. Loewe, was still our family doctor. Now a retired lawyer living near the centre of Vienna and quite close to our first flat there after our arrival from Berlin, Roland filled me in on what happened to him and his family following my last brief but memorable meeting with his mother at the Moedling Station park in July 1938, when I had told her that 'everything will be all right'.

A month after my departure from Moedling Roland had gone on a visit to Zagreb in Yugoslavia with a friend. Being only half Jewish Roland had not been subjected to any maltreatment after the Anschluss (Indeed, his best friend was a Nazi at the time, and remained his best friend till the end of his life). While Roland was away from home, his father was reported to the Nazi authorities for trying to transfer his money abroad, and so was forced to pay the 'Reich Emigration Tax' before emigrating to Brussels, leaving Frau Loewe in Moedling to look after her ailing mother.

Roland, being half Jewish, soon realised that it would be safer for him to join his father in Brussels, and continued his studies there. Both he and his father were able to evade the Gestapo after the German occupation of Belgium and until the end of the war. During that time they even managed a meeting with his mother in Luxembourg for a brief re-union. Immediately after the end of the war, Roland returned to Vienna. His father returned to Moedling in 1947, and was re-united with Roland's mother there. It was ironic that when I first returned to Moedling in 1948 and was making tentative inquiries about my Jewish friends, Roland's father and mother were already back living there virtually round the corner from my childhood home.

So why would they have returned to live in a community and a country that had persecuted them? The answer is simply that this was where they came from, and they well knew that their persecutors were only a small minority who had come to power through an accident of history. As for those who had 'looked the other way', they were part of that majority of the human race everywhere who just 'go with the flow'. Seen in the context of his own history, Roland's father had been an Austrian citizen all his life, had been a doctor in the Austrian army in the first world war, and was in any event a 'baptized' Jew who was returning to a culture and an area that had been his home for most of his life. This is where he belonged.

During a more recent visit to Moedling I inadvertently met another victim of dual belongings. Our friendly guide Frau Friederike Fida had taken us to some of the local tourist spots, and after a privileged visit (she had her own key) to the flat in the 'Beethhoven House' where he had composed the Missa Solemnis, she took us to the St.Othmar Church on top of the hill. After enquiring from a cleaner working there whether we could have the Altar lights turned on, since it was quite dark, a young priest came out of a lit-up side vestry. He knew Frau Fida, who promptly introduced us, and realising that my wife Marie spoke no German, he addressed us in perfect English. It turned out that he had been brought up in Hertford, but since his father was Viennese and had returned to Vienna, he had decided to start on an ecclesiastical career there. It brought home to me that there must be an ever-growing sector of humanity brought up in dual, and more often even multiple belongings.

The Swiss writer Charles Lewinsky has contributed a searing contemporary account of Jewish belonging in his play and film under the title *A quite ordinary Jew* (Ein ganz gewoehnlicher Jude). It is simply a soliloquy by the son of Jewish refugees who had returned to Hamburg after the war. He had been asked by an acquaintance to address a class at his local school on what it means to be a Jew in Germany. On reflection, his first response is anger. Why should he be asked to explain his particular aspect of 'being German'? Why not ask a Catholic, or a Protestant, or even a Muslim. Why him? Is it perhaps because the one thing they can't forgive the Jews is the Holocaust, and one way of making them pay is to let them know that they don't really 'belong'?

After all these years of being British in terms of my environment and culture, being 'bi-national' due to my early upbringing has given me a dichotomy with 'belonging' which presents particular difficulties with patriotism, and would help explain my affinity to 'Europeanism'. There are aspects of both British and German culture that I like, and some that I dislike. When I am in Germany or Austria I tend to promote the 'British' way, yet back 'home', although I think of myself as British, I tend to defend or promote the German or Austrian ways. The Vienna Woods and the Austrian Alps together with the music of Johann Strauss have become ingrained in my psyche, but so have the green fields and the gentle hills of England together with the music of Vaughan Williams and Elgar. I am inspired by both, and yet not patriotic, and it is extremely unlikely that I will ever join any marches for either side. If I ever do, it will be to a different drummer from the one those around me are hearing. As in my younger days in the Air Training Corps, I will continue marching straight ahead when the rest are doing a left or right wheel.

Belonging to a family, a tribe, a race, a class, a political party, a nation or a religion could arguably be said to be the origin of social ethics designed to ensure the survival of each of these entities in addition to that of the self. And yet this 'belonging' is dictated by the accidents of history responsible for placing us into a particular geographical and historical environment. For the great majority of the human race belonging to the family, followed by any of the larger associations needed to ensure its survival, is the initial common denominator.

Beyond that the increasing wealth and stability of western society has led to the formation of innumerable clubs, societies and associations where like-minded people can meet and satisfy their need to belong. Some of these, like fan and supporter clubs of football, rugby, cricket, baseball, bowles etc. may well account for more adherents than the religions.

The comforting feeling of belonging is often fuelled by strong emotions which can be harmless in themselves, unless associated with fear. Fear of others who speak and behave differently, who belong to another class, another tribe, another race, another nation, or another religion. This fear is undoubtedly one of the most common characteristics of the human race, and helps to fuel anger and aggression, a trait that goes back to medieval times when there was good cause to be afraid of others who came from afar, often with the intent to rob, rape and kill. In more recent times our leaders, when faced with flagging support, have exploited this inbred human characteristic by engendering enthusiasm for going to war with other nations by exaggerating or even falsifying the evidence of impending danger, just as Goebbels did for Hitler before Germany invaded Poland.

Being conditioned by our upbringing makes us all victims of history to varying degrees. Those who engage in rational analysis of the choices open to them at any time stand a greater chance of becoming truly human simply by freeing themselves of the shackles of prejudice inherited from their belonging. Both Hitler and Churchill were motivated by their belonging to view themselves as partaking of a mission to further what they saw as the interests of their respective nations. The principal difference between the two was that in Hitler's case his irrational prejudices bordered on derangement.

Belonging is invariably associated with emotion to a greater or lesser degree. Certainly my memory of my friends Herbert and Walter marching along under the swastika flag in the Hitler Youth squad was one of pride in belonging (in spirit at least) to what they were experiencing. Whenever this memory surfaces, it is accompanied by the Horst Wessel Nazi anthem 'Raise high the flag, with ranks tightly closed, SA marches in quiet, solid step', which was heard day after day during the Anschluss, and added incidental music to my feeling of belonging.

In later years I was assailed by similar emotions at the last nights of the Promenade Concerts at the Albert Hall in London, when it was customary for the audience to stand for the orchestra's rendering of 'Rule Britannia'. Although this might appear to be similar in sentiment to the original German National Anthem 'Germany above all in the world' (Deutschland ueber Alles in der Welt), the latter was really meant to merely imply that 'the Fatherland' was to reign supreme in the aspirations of 'us Germans', without the territorial implications of 'Rule Britannia;.

The comforting feeling of 'belonging' made me stand with the rest, but there was always a shadow of a doubt cast over my emotions. Now I am definitely unpatriotic to the extent that my loyalty is first and foremost to my fellow humans regardless of race or nationality, and my emotions are more likely to be stirred by Beethoven's 'Ode to Joy' used as the anthem of the European Union.

Political, national, religious and racist belongings have been the primary cause of human conflict in the last few centuries. Although differences of political beliefs have been accommodated within the western democracies, the more difficult ones to reconcile are the religious ones, particularly if associated with race. This should not be surprising, since religious beliefs are not concerned with reason and open to debate. They are simply the dictums of various gods as purveyed by their numerous prophets.

As long as these dictums relate to belief in the purpose of human life and rituals to please their respective gods, they may be seen as harmless. The problems arise with the great contradictions in ethics contained within the major religious scriptures which enable extremists to select those that suit their particular version of their beliefs. Thus, for example, the exhortations demanding unwavering belief from their followers, reinforced by the threat of eternal punishment in the case of Christianity and even killing of non-believers in the case of Islam.

The innate conflict between belonging to a nation and belonging to a larger entity like religion or a political belief was illustrated in the chapter 'What We Knew' by mentioning how some of the objectors to the area bombing of German and Japanese cities followed by the nuclear bombing of Hiroshima and Nagasaki were branded as being 'unpatriotic' if not downright traitors. In this instance their prime motive would have been religious, but subsequent examples of political beliefs leading to similar accusations abound in connection with communist sympathisers such as George Bernard Shaw, Bertrand Russel and Kim Philby together with his associates. In the latter case, the perpetrators actually left their homeland, since their activities had a direct bearing on British agents being uncovered and executed by the Soviet Union, so in these instances there is room for doubt as to their moral justifications.

In general, however, the conflict between patriotism and beliefs is justifiable and often, in retrospect, honourable. We would certainly have had no quarrel with those Germans who were branded unpatriotic by their government and a good proportion of their countrymen, and who lived and died in concentration camps for their unpatriotic beliefs. In the case of some exceptional individuals, the extent of their commitment to beliefs over patriotism goes even further. Einstein, for example, wrote 'The greatest obstacle to international order is that monstrously exaggerated spirit of nationalism which also goes by the fair-sounding but misused name of patriotism', and in later life 'I am truly a lone traveller and have never belonged to my country, my home, my friends or even my immediate family with my whole heart'. Yet he gave himself unsparingly to humanitarian causes such as helping Jewish refugees and various movements for promoting peace and nuclear disarmament.

For the British, a good example of an exceptional individual who spurned patriotism in favour of adherence to universal principles was Thomas Paine, whose 'The Age or Reason' broke new ground by proclaiming 'The Rights of Man', which has become one of the foundation stones on which the Universal Declaration of Human Rights by the United Nations is based. Yet Paine was regarded as a traitor and renegade in Great Britain, and even to this day is not honoured by a commemorative statue in its capital.

Charles Darwin, a more universally acknowledged and honoured Englishman, recommended that we should extend our sympathies beyond the members of our own nation to the people of all nations and races.

The nurturing of beliefs from ancient times to the present due to our need to belong is passed on from generation to generation over the centuries. Yet the primary purpose of this nurturing is to maintain social ethics that have helped the tribe or larger community to survive, and is fostered by the establishment, i.e. the dominant part of the tribe or community whose principal interest is the maintenance of the status quo. The prophets and high priests who formulated these social ethics, usually on the basis that these were given to them directly by their gods or god, as the case may be, were venerated by the establishment. They, after all, helped to keep 'the masses' under control, thus perpetuating both their beliefs and the continuance of their establishment, assisted by the revealed threat of the dire consequences to unbelievers.

In spite of having split up into countless factions and sub-factions, the survival and durability of the two principal established religions, Christianity and Islam, for nearly two millennia illustrates how 'belonging' throughout has triumphed over reason. Even in recent times when a sizeable portion of the shrinking number of believers do so in order to maintain the status quo rather than venture into the unknown, we still pay lip service to cults and customs which defy reason. Although we no longer sacrifice virgins, we still allow male and, in the Islamic world, female circumcision, both of which may have contributed to the survival of the tribe some millennia ago but are now irrelevant.

The conflict between human nature and reason is ongoing. Centuries ago Galileo was condemned to spend the last nine years of his life under house arrest because his findings of the nature of our solar system conflicted with the universe depicted in the bible. Today we have a re-play with Darwin's theory of evolution being challenged by religious movements such as the followers of Creationism and 'Intelligent Design'. We even still have the remains of a Flat Earth society inspired by yet another interpretation of the Bible, whilst the 'Hollow Earth' interpretation by the American 'Koreshan Unity Foundation', another Christian sect, has given up the ghost and is now only commemorated in a museum.

In addition, and stimulated by the growth of the internet, there is a multiplicity of esoteric beliefs and their associated groups of followers, such as the belief that the holocaust never happened. An aberration associated with 'belonging' that defies reason and is particularly ironic in view of the defeat of Hitler with his notions of racial superiority is the institution of Monarchy. The British Royal family, by tacit consent, is thereby invested with special powers and privileges simply because of its inherited genes, i.e. race. Another aberration attributable to the need to belong, both on a local and national scale, is the world-wide phenomenon of football fans and followers. One incident associated with this aberration and engraved in my mind was the spectacle of seven-year-olds at an international football game waving their country's flags and bursting into tears when their team was defeated, undoubtedly conditioned by their parents' overriding need to belong.

An aberration associated with belonging which should make us all shudder is the demonstration of military might and discipline on the occasions of anniversary celebrations of some event of national importance in the past. Few could have equalled what the Nazis achieved with their goose-stepping troops, but these arcane rituals are on-going today and might well give pause for concern, were it not for the fact that they are so grotesque they serve as a form of comic entertainment. Unfortunately a significant sector of the populations world-wide do not see them in this light, and are overcome by awe and patriotic enthusiasm for what they see as a demonstration of the safeguarding of their belonging. Another feature of these rituals that is still alive today, some 80 years after their hay day in Nazi Germany, are the athletic mass synchronisms performed by flag-waving gymnasts in huge stadiums to demonstrate how the many can all be made to move in harmony at the behest of a few.

The Ethics of Survival

Although my dual belonging has been instrumental in this work, my intention throughout has been to look at the assembled facts dispassionately before arriving at any conclusions. Having been brought up in two different cultures enables me to empathise with both, in addition to making it easier for me to empathise with the rest of humanity as well. Armed with this innate advantage coupled with the experiences gained from a lifetime in engineering, has prompted me to speculate whether we could make life more civilised for all by applying reason not only to the control of nature, but also to the control of human nature.

From the beginning of homo sapiens our beliefs have been shaped by prophets, priests, gurus, philosophers and statesmen who were engaged in attempting to control human nature, and in particular its more unsavoury traits such as greed, lust, envy, anger, violence and cruelty, to name a few. All of these could be said to fall within the scope of what we can simply define as anti-social traits.

Until recent times, religious belief has been primarily responsible for explaining the meaning and purpose of life to Homo sapiens. This explanation was coupled to a belief in an afterlife in the (un-defined) domains of either heaven or hell depending on whether it was to be reward or punishment for the extent to which we had or had not controlled our human nature in this life.

What I now propose is for us to simply put the conjectures about the ultimate meaning and purpose of life to one side, and accept that we should attempt to live a rewarding life together whether we believe in a god or not. The rewards for behaving socially and the punishments for behaving anti-socially should be in our hands, to be administered in this life, regardless of what happens in the next.

What remains is for us to agree what is socially good or bad. I don't think that this will be an insurmountable problem, except with those whose interpretation of their beliefs does not allow for any others. For these, some methods of restraint will have to be agreed.

From the first fire ever lit by homo sapiens to the development of nuclear energy, controlling nature to our benefit has been an ongoing process. What we have failed to do is to apply reason also to the control of human nature in order to safeguard our continued existence. By human nature in this context I mean human behaviour inculcated by belonging and dominated by emotion as opposed to reason. Thus, in the same way that we would put in place measures to protect ourselves from the effects of random natural catastrophes such as tornadoes, tsunamis, earthquakes, floods etc., we can use reason to prevent, or mitigate random catastrophic acts of human nature such as wars, terrorism, the persecution of minorities and the destruction of our environment.

Undeniably reason has also been applied to developing ever more efficient methods of killing our fellow humans, with ever fewer numbers of us able to kill ever larger numbers, but this I see as an example of reason used in the service of human nature rather than its control.

Human nature is largely dependent on upbringing and experiences in our formative years, all subject to random events, or, as I like to put it, accidents of history, which none of us have any control over. Thus the world view of someone born into a South American Indian tribe in a remote tropical forest will be quite different from that of a citizen of a major modern metropolis. Even in the latter case, there will be significant differences in world views between various sectors, between the masses and the establishment, the rich and the poor, as well as between different countries with different religions or beliefs.

Since our world views are shaped by events outside our control, this could be taken to mean that we have no free will, since all our actions will be the result of prejudice rather than reason. This was certainly the case in the developments leading up to the holocaust in Germany. There, the people's options of exercising free will did not apply for the simple reason that there was neither the freedom nor the desire to exercise it, since this would have resulted in jeopardising their immediate comforts or careers, and possibly their lives. But this applies to most of us still here and now. Even the writing of this book have made me debate how much of a risk I am taking in publicising my views regarding the abandonment of religious teaching in state schools in favour of the adoption of Humanist (i.e. non-religious) ethics, thus making me a possible target for religious extremists. But I am persisting, if for no other reason than to prove to the reader, and myself, that I believe that my will should be free, and damn the consequences!

Up until the beginning of the twentieth century it was generally accepted that we teach our children religion to help, cajole or threaten them to control their own natures in accordance with the edicts of their God. Since then we have begun to question religion, and are now approaching the situation where, in Western

Europe at least, the non-religious are rapidly approaching equality of numbers with the religious. The principal reason for the persistence of the religions is that 'belonging' has been embedded in the psyche of the believers. They feel bound to accept rituals and beliefs simply because their parents and their ancestors had believed in them, or because some guru influenced them to do so. Beyond that, they are reluctant to abandon the comforting belief in an afterlife that will bring them and/or their loved ones the happiness they missed out on in this life. This, they believe, is the purpose and meaning of life, which the rest of us either accept as un-knowable, or maintain that there is none..

Another reason for the reluctance of abandoning religion has been the belief that without the moral codes embedded in religious teaching, there would be no rules to govern our behaviour. My answer to this is that for those who cannot accept that the rules imposed by religion were made by God, or even gods, but by man, it only remains to make up rules we can all, or at least most of us, agree on – in short, Social Ethics.

Social ethics go back as far as the Greek philosophers from more than two millennia ago. They are based on the idea that our behaviour towards one another should be based not on pleasing a God or gods, but on helping one another to live the best and most fulfilled life possible. A good starting point is the Golden Rule 'Do unto others as you would like them to do unto you.' This, it should be noted, does not allow for exceptions for those whom you suspect of not being followers of the Rule.

Since the Golden Rule is already accepted by most religions as well as by the non-religious, it could well form the basis or underlying principle of universally acceptable Social Ethics. Extending the principle to guidelines applicable to our current social scenario will require both moral and political motivation.

Beyond that, we should refute the idea that it is desirable for us all to compete in the acquisition of wealth and/or power over others. From the very beginning of civilisation the subjugation of the self to the community has been the on-going theme of religions and philosophies, latterly particularly in connection with the idea of promoting equal rights by a more equitable sharing of wealth and power.

Extending this principle from the personal to the national scale would mean refuting the idea that it is every nation's duty to compete with other nations for the world's resources. Inevitably such competition leads to conflict, resulting in the dominance of those nations better armed and more ruthless in subjugating other nations. This is what Hitler understood by the survival of the fittest, and he was by no means the last to promulgate the idea that Darwin's theory of evolution should provide us with guidance on how we should live. The obvious flaw in this view is that although species do compete to survive, members of any one species tend to co-operate to ensure its survival, and thus their own.

Arriving at some agreed syllabus for Social Ethics can be seen to be a reasonable approach towards a world where mutual assured destruction is relegated to mutual assured survival. The current world situation is one of national and international political and religious conflict, often accompanied by the persecution of minorities. A move towards some form of international agreement on what we teach our children at school about both inter-personal and international social behaviour is in my view therefore of the utmost importance.

This is of particular relevance in the current situation, where the growth of competition and the internet has left the coming generation at the mercy of commercial pressures in the formation of their world views. At the same time the pressures on parents to compete leaves little if any time for conversing with their offspring on anything beyond how to deal with their immediate needs or desires. Apart from what they learn at school, their early upbringing is influenced by what they see and hear on TV, the internet and their digital play stations. TV is dominated by commercial pressures aimed at what the providers think will get them the largest viewership, with very little of relevance in giving our offspring some consensus on what we, as parents, value. With the internet, the intrusion of commercial pressures is at least modified by the discourse between similar age and interest groups via social media such as face book, twitter and the rest, but still leaves the question of what, if anything, the parents should contribute.

First and foremost will be for us to have some input to what the social ethics syllabus will consist of, in addition to acquainting ourselves with it to enable us to communicate with our offspring on issues arising from this on a day to day basis. A good example of this would be the question of why, and how, they should respect their elders. It is worth noting here that the trend towards teaching children to arrive at their own conclusions on matters of this kind from an early age should take second place to teaching them what we believe. Any form of teaching involves some discipline and even coercion, such as penalties for absconding from school lessons. Nor would teachers be able to fulfil their functions if every other rule of their subjects is questioned and dissected. This priviledge will come later when their pupils have completed their education.

In order to reduce the likelihood of a repeat of 'the war', teaching our children the importance of our belonging to the human family over just belonging to our nation or family is of the utmost importance. Of equal importance will be to do so from the very beginning, rather than leaving a vacuum to be filled either by commercial pressures dominated by the latest fashions in everything or the rants of un-reason.

The first step along this journey will be to remove religion from our educational syllabuses and replace it with Social Ethics. Just condensing these into universally acceptable rules governing human social intercourse, both on a personal and international level, will form a very important foundation stone to put into the vacuum we have at the moment. Religious Education (i.e the origins and contents of the various religions) can then be incorporated in the history syllabus, and religious observance removed from state schools entirely and put into the hands of the existing religious bodies.

Arriving at an acceptable basis for Social Ethics will involve appointing representatives of the major religions and other beliefs such as humanism and atheism, to draw up a consensual statement of values and guidelines for social behaviour. Once adopted, these will remain subject to regular scrutiny and revision in the same way as our legal system. Extending the same principle internationally, i.e. agreeing on rules of international behaviour based on the same Social Ethics, will do no more than consolidate the already widely held belief that we all jointly share a brief sojourn on spaceship earth, and should all cooperate to make this as good as possible for all of us.

There have been notable moves in the direction of introducing ethics to take the place of religious instruction worldwide. The British Secular Society, the British Humanist Association, the Rationalist Press Association, International Humanist and Ethical Union, the American Humanist Association and numerous other Humanist groups worldwide have all been engaged in getting Humanist values introduced in their countries. They have gained access to their media and governments, and have been successful in influencing legislation. In Britain, for example, they helped to repeal the Blasphemy laws, and are engaged in trying to stop the spreading of Free Academy schools used as indoctrination bases for sectarian beliefs.

There are in addition other movements aiming to introduce ethics into mainstream thinking, such as the 'Scientists for Global Responsibility' in Britain and the 'Global Ethic Foundation' in Germany. In Australia there have been moves in this direction in the state of New South Wales, where 'Primary Ethics' is now taught in some 300 schools as an alternative to religion, and in Victoria, where the Humanist Society is recruiting volunteers to run Secular Ethics classes in state primary schools.

Getting international; agreements on the teaching of Social Ethics will be the next step, and on the face of it an insurmountable one. However, the ground is already prepared for this by the adoption by the United Nations of the 'International Declaration of Human Rights' in 1947, just over 150 years after Thomas Paine's polemic entitled 'Rights of man'. These rights are still not much more than an ideal to aim at, as the Articles listed below demonstrate:

> Article 1. All human beings are born free and equal in dignity and rights ....
>
> Article 23. (1) Everyone has the right to work ....

Nevertheless, they may well be incorporated as fundamental values in Social Ethics, coupled with others to be democratically agreed by qualified panels, with some give and take between factions. This give and take would apply principally to the world views, i.e. religion versus humanism, followed by the political views, i.e. left versus right, or the balance between the state and the individual.

The sort of situation where the application of Social Ethics could make a difference in international affairs, is our unquestioning acceptance that our immediate financial well-being has to take preference over any ethical considerations. Britain's arms deals with Saudi Arabia in recent history are a good example of sacrificing long term principle for immediate financial gain. The fact that Saudi Arabia has since been reputed to help finance the extreme Muslim Isis faction should give us cause for reflection. So should the spectacle of Prince Charles being welcomed on a good-will mission to Saudi Arabia at a time when public floggings of anti-government bloggers were still going on there, and whilst the death penalty for homosexual activities remains in force.

A move towards federalism in the EU should be welcomed as a means to promoting ethical beliefs acceptable to all the members of the union. On the global scale, the UN is already moving in this direction by putting pressure on those member nations that persistently ignore the Human Rights Charter.

Going on from the above, keeping the peace between member states should progressively be put under the control of a United Nations police authority with national branches in the member states responsible to it. A first step in this direction has been taken by the formation of the United Nations peacekeeping force, which has until now been used exclusively to protect minority elements in its member states from persecution. The next step should be the transfer of the control of national armies to an international police force, accompanied by the dismantling of nuclear weapons of all member states. The pooling of arms and personnel involved should also help to reduce the scale and power of the international arms trade and lead to the eventual abandonment of all nuclear weapons.

On the positive side, the United Nations through its various agencies has been instrumental in ameliorating the sufferings of millions due to starvation, disease or strife. Even on the issue of climate change, there is now a growing global movement towards emissions agreements on limiting CO_2.

This issue has now reached crisis point, and within the context of us saving our planet for future generations, Social Ethics will have to incorporate a section on how we should all behave in order to make this possible. As Naomi Klein, the Canadian reporter and author, comments in *This Changes Everything*[37]: 'For any of this to change, a world view will need to rise to the fore that sees nature, other nations, and our own neighbors not as adversaries, but rather as partners in a grand project of reinvention.'

When it comes to measures to prevent a recurrence of the Holocaust, these again have to be adopted globally, since the basic causes, poverty and inequality, exist globally, and will lead to conflict either in the form of international or civil conflict, particularly where nationalist, religious or political extremists are able to exploit the situation.

In a world that is shrinking by the day due to the explosive rise in communications and trade, our sense of belonging will of necessity need to change as well, and the importance of national interests will have to give way to international interests, a step not that dissimilar from the previous step from city states to nations. To facilitate this change, the adoption of common Social Ethics will be necessary for the realisation of the Rights of Man, the next step after the Declaration which was its founding stone.

Epilogue

Humanists have gone some way towards proclaiming their ultimate goal to be simply to make their lives and those of their fellow humans as happy and fulfilled as possible. Since they don't believe in a life after death, this remains their ultimate purpose.

One aspect of the question of belief is the extent to which our origins and upbringing influences what we believe. Although Fred and I were brought up in the German Protestant belief, my parents were basically non-believers, and never discussed religion with us. As part of the Austrian state education syllabus we were excused from attending the catholic instruction lessons at school subject only to attending lessons on the religion of our parents' choice instead, at venues provided by the other religious authorities concerned, in practice either Protestantism or Judaism.

My parent's decided that Protestantism was at least slightly closer to agnosticism, which in those days would have been unacceptable, so they opted for that. I thus found myself a pupil of pastor Mueller of the local Protestant Church, who often used the opportunity to let us know that he expected to see us in Church on Sundays. He tended to get irritated by my lame excuses, and on one occasion went as far as gently swiping my head with a Bible. But I seldom went, because Sunday mornings were reserved for the family outing to the Moedling indoor swimming pool, usually followed by lunch at a restaurant just up the road from where we lived called Fasching, after the local butcher who owned and ran it. Just occasionally I went to Sunday School on Sunday afternoons at the Protestant Church, usually conducted by one of the Church Elders. And one Christmas I actually recall my parents being present in the congregation when I had been cajoled to take part in the Christmas Nativity performance, in the very minor role of one of the shepherds, requiring neither vocal nor significant acting ability. Undoubtedly they had been persuaded to attend for no other reason than to support me in an activity I had personally agreed to engage in. I don't recall Fred ever attending church, nor how old I was when I ceased to believe in the Christian Religion, but it was probably between the ages of 10 and 13.

Neither of my parents ever commented on religion in our presence, and did not appear to have any concern about what we believed. They knew I was a bookworm, and that I sometimes picked up and read the books they had finished, which would have been rather unsuitable for a child. After we came to England I would repeat this practice, particularly during the war when father belonged to a book club which meant we had new books to read by current authors, such as Graham Greene and Somerset Maugham. This coincided with my becoming a member of the local library which enabled me to catch up on philosophy in order to find some anchor when it came to belief. Over many years I continued my search for this, and had no overriding belief except my non-belief in religion.

Now I have accepted that our upbringing alone was bound to have had a lasting influence, as indeed does the culture and history of our countries. Looking at the history of beliefs since the rise of Homo sapiens shows that these have changed considerably over the centuries, from the days when we worshipped many gods and placated them with human sacrifices, to today when the principal religions, Christianity, Islam, Hinduism and Buddhism account for some 79% of believers worldwide, with the remainder split between numerous other beliefs including a 16% and rapidly growing sector of non-believers.

The rise of a belief in a single god as opposed to a multiplicity only goes back to the birth of Judaism, a minute fraction of the time since the beginning of homo sapiens some 200,000 years ago. At the time that the idea of a single god took root, humans still believed their immediate environment was the ultimate centre of humanity, with the sky arching over it in a gigantic hemisphere. It wasn't until around 300 BC, just 2300 years ago, that the earth was mooted to be a sphere, and only just over 400 that it rotated around the sun which was the centre of the universe. And now we know that our sun is just one of billions, with only a minute proportion visible to the human eye and known as stars.

None of these facts had any influence on humanity's major religious beliefs until relatively recently, when more believers realised that their god had never mentioned any of this to his prophets, resulting in some modifications of interpretations of the Bible and the Koran, the major religious works. Even now the fact that our earth is not the centre of the universe has not been incorporated into any of the religions. However, the exponential growth of science over the last few centuries has been followed by an exponential decline in religious believers, resulting in the likely reduction of the number of gods worshipped from 1 to zero, no doubt accompanied by an increase of the killings fostered by the remaining extremist religious elements which have arisen over the last twenty years.

In the meantime global warming, and now the spread of the coronavirus, has given us all a jolt. Recent forecasts about the future of mankind, such as those by Steven Pinker in *The Better Angels of Our Nature* or Noah Yuval Harari in *Homo Deus – A Brief History of Tomorrow* took the continued survival of humanity for the foreseeable future for granted. Now we are shaken by how optimistic these assumptions are.

Our unexpected exposure to the new plague jolted my memory back to my schooldays in Moedling, and the popular folk song we were taught about the legendary Augustin, the hero of the great plague of Vienna in 1679. The first verse of the song just about says it all. It goes:

> Oh my dear Augustin, Augustin, Augustin,
> oh my dear Augustin, everything is 'hin'

('hin' is the German colloquial for 'gone phut', which I put here because it rhymes).

Augustin was a popular street musician, his instrument being a bagpipe. At the height of the plague, having lost most of his friends, he is drowning his sorrows at his local pub late one evening, the last customer. He staggers out on to the road and promptly passes out. The gang of workers employed to remove any stray bodies found on the streets load him up as just another corpse and take him out to the plague pits outside Vienna. When he wakes up in the morning lying on a heap of bodies in the pit he starts calling for help. No one hears, so he gets out his bagpipe and blows it as hard as he can. He is rescued and spends the remaining fifteen years of his life entertaining his fellow Viennese with his music. They all believed it was the alcohol in his body that had saved him from becoming a victim.

The Corona Virus has also jolted British Evangelists into action. One of their pamphlets with the title *Hope beyond Coronavirus* finishes with the admonition that p*erhaps we should take the Coronavirus as a loving warning* (from God, of course!) *to a rebellious world.* As one of the rebels I would comment that if this is his love, what would his hate be like?

Whatever the chances of the long term survival of our species may be, the current situation at least puts more pressure on believers and non-believers to agree on the adoption of some form of consensus Social Ethics designed to make this more likely. The most important aspect of any such move will be to stop the teaching of any religion as part of our education curriculum other than in the context of history, in the same way as we deal with politics and philosophy. This would also entail moving the observance and practice of religions into the private sector, with parents entitled to arrange this for their children until these reach an agreed maturity age.

Such a proposal seems perfectly logical to me, but the obstacles to getting it accepted are of course immense in view of the fact that humanists at present still account only for a small minority of beliefs. A rational explanation of the reasons for the continuing dominance of the religions can simply be this: religious believers need not be rational. Their beliefs are based on their god or founder, as reported by their prophets, so need not be justified by mere human reason. The durability of the major religions, with Christianity topping the list with some 33% of the world population, is in my view due to the fact that the establishments of the nations involved found it easier to maintain their power over their fellow countrymen by aligning themselves with the existing religions rather than try introducing new ones.

Although still basically a Humanist, which implies that I do not believe there is any purpose in life other than trying to achieve the greatest possible happiness for myself and for my fellow humans, I would now have to amend this in view of current statistics, which indicate that a majority of humans are either suffering from physical pain, disease, depression, hunger, dementia, madness and war, with a good proportion of the remainder engaged in simply killing those who do not follow their beliefs or have abandoned them. In addition there is the random suffering due to birth defects, physical or mental disabilities, not to mention natural disasters caused by storms, floods and earthquakes.

After all that, I think that the main aim of humanism should be to reduce human suffering, which could be regarded as a monumental task, though not as great as that of making us all happy, which for most of us will anyway be a very temporary state usually balanced by periods of unhappiness, except in the case of the mentally retarded. So I believe that a more achievable ethical aim would be that of ensuring that as many of us as possible can live a life free of pain, if not full of pleasure, and free of stress if not full of boredom.

It could be argued that this ethical aim is already adopted by a majority of our fellow humans, subject to the qualification that for most of us it dominates our activities only in as far as it applies to ourselves, followed in diminishing degrees to members of our family, then members of our clan, then our nation, and only finally the rest of humanity. I would even go as far as to say that for most of us what we do to reduce pain and stress for the rest of humanity is very little if anything. This also applies to the religious beliefs, whose ultimate aim is after all only to gain the approval of our god or gods who say little, if anything, about us helping to keep our fellow humans free from pain and stress.

Nevertheless, there are still many of us committed to supporting international organisations such as the United Nations and Medicins Sans Frontieres who do just that. When it comes to getting the United Nations to agree on measures that would eliminate ongoing conflicts worldwide, however, we know that we have not had much success.

Nearing the end of a long and varied life, I am more aware than ever of my lack of any commitment to a belief which could give a clear and simple answer to the question of what it has all been about. The rationalist (and principally scientific) view of our universe does not concern itself with this kind of question. We are bombarded with TV documentaries conducted by what are obviously revered and intelligent scientists who tell us about black holes and exploding numbers of universes in addition to ours, separated by an infinite time scale, and are expected to accept that it all started some billions of years ago and will disappear into another black hole after an infinity of time. My immediate question then goes something like ‘Hold on, even a black hole must have had something to make a hole in, and what is that?’ And furthermore, what is infinity, and what is nothingness? Since none of us can comprehend either, how can we accept any explanations using these terms?

On the opposite side we have proponents of beliefs which in my view beggar belief. They have a simple answer to the question of purpose. It must be to please their god, or gods, who have communicated their wishes to us through the various prophets mentioned in their respective tomes. Problem solved, at least as far as they are concerned!

The above may suffice to confirm that I am not a believer, certainly not in religion. I do believe, however, that as far as we know at present, we humans are the only cognitive being in our universe, and my mission, if any, has been to promote the welfare and continuation of our species with what little power and intelligence I possess.

We have now been in the grip of the corona pandemic for almost two years, and although the prospects of finding a release from it are improving, it has brought us up against the fact that there may be other and more serious viruses lurking. The only positive aspect might be that the great majority of our species who still believed in a god who has our interests at heart or wherever he might keep them must be beginning to waver, hopefully resulting in a surge towards atheism or agnosticism.

So exactly what should social ethics consist of? Up to now our ethics in the western world have been loosely based on Christianity, and our legal system on the ethics derived from it. As I see it, social ethics should be principally concerned with how humans behave to one another, and will not deal with wider issues such as the meaning or purpose of life. These matters should be left to the followers of various religions, or atheists and humanists to decide for themselves, except on the issue of the relationship between these factions of humanity. The single most prominent issue is that of the intolerance of extremist elements of these factions who believe they should kill people simply for defecting from their belief to another, or worse still, to kill them simply for belonging to another religion. Their justification for doing so can be based on interpretations of segments of the written basis of some religions, such as the Bible or the Koran.

One of the principal rules of current social ethics is based on the simple admonition from the Bible: 'do unto others as you would have them do unto you', often misinterpreted with 'as you would expect them to do unto you'. It is in any case rather variable, and should in my view be changed to 'Do not kill or engage in any activity that may cause pain or suffering to others', a somewhat diminished admonition from the current Humanist one of aiming to achieve the greatest happiness for the greatest number.

The reader might ask how I have managed to live a reasonably happy life without ever knowing what its ultimate purpose was. The answer must be that the happier parts outweighed the unhappy parts to an extent that this question seldom surfaced in my mind. In retrospect I think that I have been happiest after succeeding to make others happy, not a frequent occurrence. On a lesser scale, satisfaction with a job done well ranks pretty highly. Pleasure again ranks lower than happiness, and is achievable for most of us, ranging from the purely physical to the emotional. The effect on the emotions of the arts, and in particular music, can be pleasurable even though sad emotions are often involved. Perhaps the net pleasurable effect is due to the knowledge that we are empathizing emotionally with countless other fellow humans, which could be argued is not that different from loving others.

Empathizing with family and friends is taken for granted, but extending our empathy beyond that to other races, nations and religions is not. Being a son of two nations has made me more aware of this problem, particularly in connection with immigrants. It is of course the first step towards the idea that we all belong to the same world, now in particular when all of us are threatened by worldwide problems such as global warming and the Corona virus pandemic, which can only be solved by at least a majority of UN member nations working together.

As a supporter of the United Nations Association in the UK I believe we should be proposing the adoption of consensus social ethics in the form of an addition to the 17 Sustainable Development Goals of the UN, with the objective that these should be based on promoting humanity's chances of survival rather than pleasing any particular god or gods. This proposal should be accompanied by the directive that membership of the UN executive should be restricted to secular nations – a pretty ambitious step. But who knows, it might all happen yet! Finally, although humanity will continue to be the victim of random events, this should not stop us from taking whatever steps we can to reduce the likelihood of a demise of our species. Since we have not been able to contact any equivalent intelligence in the universe, our principal aim should be to preserve and promote our highest achievements in science and the arts. Consensus Social Ethics will be the essential tool required to do that. On an emotional and artistic note, I will end my diatribe by recommending Beethoven's Ode to Joy as means of achieving pleasure without pain!

Reference Works

1 Ausgeloescht (Extinguished) Mail Edition Umbruch, A-240 Moedling, 1988
2 Peter Weiser, *Wien stark bewoelkt* (Vienna overcast) 1984 Christian Brandstaetter, Vienna-Munich
3 Kershaw, Ian: *Hitler, the Germans and the final solution.* Yale University Press 2008
4 Johnson, Eric *What we knew: Terror, Mass Murder and Everyday Life in Nazi Germany* Libri & Basic Books, Cambridge, Mass. USA 2005
5 Hans Fallada: *Alone in Berlin.* Penguin Classics 2009
6 BBC Broadcast in German 1944
7 Fest, Joachim: *Not me* London:Atlantic 2011
8 Sereny, Gitta: *The German Trauma* London: Allen Lane 2000
9 Sereny, Gitta: *Albert Speer* London: Macmillan 1995
10 Treblinka
11 Michael H Kater *Composers of the Nazi Era: Eight Portraits* Oxford University Press 1999
12 Ulrike Migdal *Ilse Weber – Wenn wohl das Leid ein Ende hat,* (Ilse Weber – When will the suffering end)[12], Carl Hanser Verlag Muenchen.2008
13 Traudl Junge: *Until the final hour.* Weidenfeld & Nicolson 2003
14 Christabel Bielenberg: *The Road ahead,* Bantham Press 1992
15 Richard Breitman *The Architect of Genocide – Himmler and the Final Solution* The Bodley Head, London 1991
16 Mark Mazower *Hitler's Empire: Nazi Rule in Occupied Europe* Allen Lane 2008
17 (15) Henry Metelmann *Through Hell for Hitler* Spellmount, Staplehurst 1990
18 Klaus von Bismarck *Aufbruch aus Pommern (Departure from Pommern)* R.Piper GmbH Munich1992
19 Paul Berry & Mark Bostridge *Vera Brittain – A life* Chatto & Windus 1995
20 Christabel Bielenberg *The Past is myself* Chatto & Windus 1968
21 Stefan Zweig *The World of Yesterday* Cassell and Company 1943
22 William L. Shirer *The Rise and Fall of the Third Reich* Secker & Warburg Ltd 1960
23 Wladislaw Szpilman *The Pianist* Victor Gollancz 1999

24 Wilfried Daim: *Der Mann der Hitler die Ideen gab.(The man who gave Hitler the ideas)* Ueberreiter – Vienna 1984.
25 A.N.Wilson *Winifred and Wolf*, Hutchinson 2007
26 Houston Chamberlain *The Foundations of the 19th Century* Bodley Head 1913
27 Alan Bullock *Hitler – A Study in Tyrrany* Pelican Books 1962
28 Irene Harand *Sein Kampf (His Struggle – The Answer to Hitler from Irene Harand),* Self Publication, Vienna 1935, Reprinted as *Hitler's Lies,* Jaico Publishing 2010
29 Ian Kershaw *Hitler 1889-1936 Hubris* The Penguin Press 1998
30 Steven Pinker *The Better Angels of our Nature* Allen Lane/Penguin Books 2011
31 Gitta Sereny *Into that Darkness* London: Pimlico 1995
32 Richard Toye *Churchill's Empire* London: Macmillan 2010
33 Adrian Fort *Prof – the life of Frederic Lindemann* London: Jonathan Cape 2003
34 Richard Overy *The Bombing War: Europe 1939-1945* Allen Lane 2013
35 Soenke Neitzel and Harald Welzer *Soldaten – on Fighting, Killing and Dying* Simon & Schuster 2012
36 Eric Schlosser *Command and Control* Allen Lane 2013
37 Naomi Klein *This Changes Everything*, Allen Lane, Penguin Books London 2014
38 Yuval Noah Harari *Sapiens – A Brief History of Humankind* Harvill Secker, London 2014

CPSIA information can be obtained
at www.ICGtesting.com
Printed in the USA
LVHW031321180522
719028LV00022B/521

9 781803 810379